PERSONAL FINANCE
& INVESTING

PERSONAL FINANCE & INVESTING

How Anyone Can Make More, Spend Less, and Invest Wisely

KYLE LANDIS-MARINELLO

Purple Bear
Press

Personal Finance and Investing:
How Anyone Can Make More, Spend Less, and Invest Wisely

Published in the United States by Purple Bear Press LLC.
ISBN: 978-1-7371355-0-0

Cover and book design by Brian P. Graphic Arts, brianpgraphics.com

PRAISE for Personal Finance and Investing

"So many finance books are full of fluff, but NOT this one. Kyle is chock-full of actionable ideas on how to immediately save more money (you won't want to miss his 17 'Free Money Tips'). Highly recommend!"

> — Rachel Richards, Bestselling Author of *Money Honey*

"Kyle takes you through some easy wins that can help kickstart your financial success and show you this stuff really works. He illustrates—with real dollars—the impact these easy wins can have on your current and future bottom line."

> — Mindy Jensen, Co-Host of the Award-Winning *BiggerPockets Money Podcast*

"Landis-Marinello provides explanation and practical tips to help you earn more, spend less, and invest wisely. If you incorporate even half of the information in this book, you'll soon think of your money not as a burden, but as a tool to help you shape your happiest life."

> — David Q. Baughier, Curator of Fiology

"An entertaining and comprehensive guide to finding your financial independence. There's no finger-wagging or suggestions that switching to single-ply toilet paper will lead to wealth in these pages. Instead, you'll find excellent advice on the two aspects of money that are under your control: earning more and spending less. Kyle guides you through the decisions you'll need to make to decrease your spending, increase your investments, and retire relatively early, all while enjoying the things that are most important to you."

> — Emily Guy Birken, Author of *The 5 Years Before You Retire*

"Start here. Kyle offers dozens of specific actions to make more money and cut your wasted spending. (You decide what's wasted.) Once you're saving more, he explains the easiest ways to invest and grow your wealth. While you're boosting your financial independence, you'll appreciate Kyle's epic stories of his dad's amazing financial mishaps."

> — Doug Nordman, co-author (with his daughter) of *Raising Your Money-Savvy Family For Next Generation Financial Independence*

"Personal Finance and Investing is a great starting point for someone who is looking to get their finances in order. There are no gimmicks and no guilt trips. Just simple, straightforward advice that is clearly organized and succinctly explained. It is also a great book for those who are new to the FIRE (Financial Independence, Retire Early) movement, and want to dip their toes in without being told they have to live off of ramen noodles for the next decade. There are also some great resources listed throughout the book for those who want to dig deeper."

— Crystal Parker Duffy, Author of *Retirement for Teachers*

"There are A LOT of boring personal finance books out there. Kyle's book is not one of them. His writing style is honest, relatable, and engaging. At the same time, this book is packed with all the information you need to get started on your journey to financial success and FIRE. There's not a single boring or redundant chapter in it. Highly recommend!"

— Aaminah Amin, Bestselling Author of *It's Not Common Cent$*

"Kyle's combination of humorous anecdotes and succinct writing style engages the reader from cover to cover. *Personal Finance and Investing* is a comprehensive and entertaining guide for anyone on the path to Financial Independence."

— Stephen Baughier, Founder of the personal finance retreat CampFI

DEDICATION

To the family that raised me (my mom, dad, brother, and sister), and the family that is still trying to make a proper adult of me (my partner and three wonderful kids). These eight people have given me memories and laughs worth more than all the money in the world.

Get the Free Bonus Checklist

As a thank-you for buying my book, I've prepared an up-to-date checklist of all 17 of the "Free Money Tips" that appear in this book. You can download it for free at:

personalfinanceauthor.com

CONTENTS

FOREWORD

T he FIRE movement (financial independence, retire early) is gaining traction in the US and abroad, but so much attention is placed on the "RE" (retire early) part. Quitting your job to sail off into the sunset sounds so amazing — especially if you dislike your job or your supervisor. But retiring early shouldn't be the focus. The "FI" (financial independence) part is much more important, though often overlooked.

Maybe because it sounds like it's boring or too much work. Or maybe because the proposed method to attain financial independence usually doesn't make any sense or isn't applicable to your specific situation. Personal finance is personal and there isn't a one-size-fits-all approach.

However, there are many common denominators in the process:

- Spend less than you earn.
- Save and intelligently invest the remainder.
- Increase income whenever possible.

Kyle takes you through some easy wins that can help kickstart your financial success and show you this stuff really works. He illustrates — with real dollars — the impact these easy wins can have on your current and future bottom line.

Financial independence is attainable for everyone, but you WILL need to make changes to what you're doing now in order to make it work. Small tweaks to how you're handling your money can have an ENORMOUS impact down the road. Investing small amounts of money consistently can have a snowball effect. Compound interest is your best friend.

But none of this helps you if you aren't ready, willing, and able to do the work.

Kyle tells you what needs to be done and shows you how to do it — but the rest is up to you. None of this will happen if you don't do the work. Lucky for you, the work isn't that hard.

In my time as the co-host of the *BiggerPockets Money Podcast*, I've interviewed hundreds of people who are at varying steps on their own journey to financial independence. Not one person ever won the lottery or inherited their financial independence.

The people I've spoken to all have many things in common in their success:

- They all spent less than they earned.

- They all saved and intelligently invested the remainder.
- They all increased their income whenever possible.

In fact, not one person was "passive" in their approach to their finances. The common thread for every individual I've ever spoken to about their financial journey was intentionality. Every single person is intentional with their money. Being conscious of your financial situation has the biggest impact on your success.

Intentionally spending your money — and intentionally saving and investing — will literally change your life. This book will show you exactly how to do that and more. Now get out there and start your FI journey!

- Mindy Jensen

A NOTE FROM THE AUTHOR

Y ou will not be able to quit your job right after you read this. But you will have the tools to put your financial house in order. Money can stop controlling your life and stressing you out all the time.

As soon as you finish reading this book, you'll be on your way to FIRE (financial independence, retire early). Or at least to what I call FIRRE (financial independence, retire relatively early).

By "relatively," I mean retiring earlier than you would if you choose to keep doing what you're currently doing.

If you read this book and implement just a few of the ideas here, you'll be making more, spending less, and investing more wisely. You'll know how long you have to keep working before you can retire. And that retirement date will be a lot sooner than you think.

This book provides specific, actionable ways to improve your finances. My guess is that you are already smart and have good self-control. Most personal finance books assume the opposite. They're written for Homer Simpson. Those books say that to get rich and retire early, all you need to do is follow a certain formula, plan, or blueprint. Or maybe it's a 7-step or 9-step strategy. It's always an odd number of steps for some reason. And there's always at least one step that doesn't make any sense at all, like telling you to wear reindeer-print socks every day.

To be clear, there is a lot to be said for those books. And the psychology behind this is real — a systematic approach can help you build confidence and start saving money when you might otherwise have gone further into debt. There is also fascinating psychological research about how to get people to save for retirement. My favorite study is one that used photoshop to show people what they'll look like a few decades from now. After staring at pictures of their greying selves, they were inclined to save more for retirement.

People can improve their finances greatly through systematic planning and psychological tricks to make better choices. Most of us make more wrong financial choices than right ones, so it is great when any book gets someone to clean up their act in any way.

But my problem with those books is that they tend to be quite patronizing. They focus on how to help people get out of debt and obtain financial prosperity despite immense mental impairment. They provide helpful graphs like the following:

STRATEGY	OUTCOME
Mismanaging your money	Bad
Managing your money	Good

You will not see any graphs like that in this book.

This book takes a different approach. I'm not writing this for Homer Simpson. I'm writing it for you. I'm assuming that you will make the right choice when given the right information.

I'm not going to teach you how to Jedi mind-trick yourself into getting out of debt and saving more money. I'm not going to teach you how to hide money from yourself by setting up separate bank accounts in North Dakota and never looking at them. I'm not even going to recommend you track your spending or create a budget.

This book is focused on providing you good information. Once you have that information, it will be up to you to decide what to do with it.

Before we go any further, I've got a few disclaimers to make. (Hey, I'm a lawyer, so what do you expect?) Please read the copyright page of this book. As noted there, I'm writing this book entirely in my personal capacity. Also, I am not a professional accountant, financial advisor, or tax specialist. This book and everything in it is for general informational purposes only. Nothing in here substitutes for consulting with a professional.

By now you're probably wondering, "Wait, if this guy has to give that many disclaimers, then why the hell am I reading his book?" Fair point. I won't blame you if you return this book now. (Really — see my later chapter on returning products that don't meet expectations.)

But let me tell you three things you'll get out of this book that you cannot get anywhere else.

First, the information in here comes from personal experience that helped me improve my family's finances by $300,000 in one year. This did not come from being wealthy or from compromising our family's values. I'm a public interest lawyer, after all, and for most of my career, our family of five has lived off a total household income of around $50,000. Our family also values protecting the environment, and in this book, you'll see that many environmentally friendly choices are also the best choices for your finances. Our family's $300,000 change in our financial situation came from receiving forgiveness of federal student loans, refinancing our home and private student loans, and using many of the other tips in this book for how to make more, spend less, and invest wisely.

Second, this book gathers the best information available and puts it all in one place. It's one-stop shopping for information about personal finance and investing. The techniques and strategies here come from an enormous amount of research. Before writing this book, I read, watched, or listened to countless books, websites, podcasts, blogs, and videos about personal finance and the FIRE movement. I've spent many hours sifting through all of this material to bring you the very best information available. I hate it when people waste my time, so I'm not going to waste yours.

Third, you'll have fun reading this book. Not because of me or anything I've done, but because of my dad and the stories you'll soon read about him. Every anecdote in here is true, and they all come with an important financial lesson. If you find reading those stories even half as entertaining as they were when I was living them, you'll get some good laughs. Enjoy!

- Kyle

INTRODUCTION

"**D**ad, why are you getting a manicure?"

My dad and I were eating lunch together and had taken out our calendars. We were picking a date when we would meet again. The date I suggested wasn't going to work because my dad had an appointment to get his nails done.

This was confusing because my dad wears Crocs and sweatpants. I've never known him to care one bit about his appearance.

"I heard an interview with Michael Jordan," he explained. "Jordan was asked what was the best part about having unlimited amounts of money, and his answer was manicures. So I figured I'd try it out."

That's my dad. I couldn't waste as much money as he does if I tried. One of his favorite expressions is, "If you've got a problem, use the Texan solution — throw money at it and see if it goes away." Nearest I can tell, there is no such thing as a "Texan solution." If there is, my dad is the only one I know who actually subscribes to the idea that throwing money at a problem will make it go away.

It's not as though he's stupid. In fact, he's brilliant. He skipped two grades in high school and went to Harvard at the age of 16. He then became a successful psychologist and ran a private practice for decades. He has a doctorate and people call him "Dr. Neil."

But he is terrible with money. Even his decision to attend Harvard was a horrendous financial choice. Princeton had offered him a full ride. But he thought they were too preppy, so he turned down the full scholarship to Princeton. He *really* likes his sweatpants. Harvard offered him nothing. It would be 40 years before he'd finish paying off his student loans.

You're going to hear a lot about my dad. He has made nearly every financial mistake in the book. He's also wildly entertaining.

Before I dive into more stories about my dad's many financial flubs, I should mention that my parents are two of the most caring people I know. Most of their financial problems stem from wanting to provide me and my siblings with the best childhoods possible. They have always had unending generosity. Also, I love both of my parents dearly. Although my dad is not good with money, he is great at being a dad. I wouldn't change a thing about him. Mom, I love you too, and my deepest apologies if any of the stories in here embarrass you. Please forgive me. I won't give the same apology to my dad because I've yet to find anything that embarrasses him. I'm still trying.

Speaking of which, let's get back to my dad and his financial woes. Although we never talked much about money growing up, my parents actually taught my siblings and me much more than I realized. Most of these lessons were, of course, about what *not* to do.

For instance, we learned that you should always talk with your partner before making large purchases. This lesson came when my mom arrived home from work one day to find a new pinball machine in our basement. My dad had never asked my mom about making this purchase, even though it cost thousands of dollars.

And it was not just any pinball machine. It was an Elvira machine, with a life-sized picture of the scantily-clad woman from Transylvania. When you hit certain targets with the pinball, Elvira's voice boomed out inappropriate innuendos. The right combination got her to make the sounds of someone being, let's just say, aroused. To my mom, who grew up in a midwestern Protestant family, Elvira was not a welcome addition to our house.

What is most amazing about this story is that it is only the *second-worst* decision my dad ever made involving a pinball machine. (You'll read about the worst one in the "PLAN Your Meals and Snacks" chapter.)

Why am I telling you all of these stories about my dad? Because he's the one who taught me that you need much more than raw intelligence to be good with money. My dad is living proof of that. He's one of the smartest people I know, but that hasn't helped his finances.

Personal finance is not one-size-fits-all. Let me give you two quick examples of why conventional wisdom is not always the best advice:

(1) Most financial advisors say that you should never buy a house until you can make at least a 20% down payment. My partner and I bought our house with *no* money down. In fact, our mortgage involved 103% financing so that we would be able to cover closing costs. This was the right financial choice for us because the house was underpriced. We were able to lock in a low 3.5% interest rate and start building equity for around the same amount we were already paying in rent every month.

(2) Many financial advisors tell you to minimize student loans and to pay them off as quickly as possible. When I got my law degree, I did exactly the opposite for my federal loans. It was the right financial choice for me. Thanks to a program known as Public Service Loan Forgiveness, I'll never actually pay in full the hundreds of thousands of dollars I took out in student loans.

So you can see why I'm skeptical of one-size-fits-all advice on personal finance. Also, those approaches often provide directly contradictory advice. One book says you have to lower all your expenses and live frugally. The next says you should buy everything you want so you keep a "rich mindset" that motivates you to make more money. Both cannot be right.

The one-size-fits-all approach is too simplistic. Yet at the same time, financial advisors often over-complicate matters by directing people to take specific steps at specific times of their lives. We are left feeling like we'll never get our finances in order if we miss a single step. But personal finances do not actually work that way.

The basic formula for personal finances is, in fact, incredibly simple. Let me start with a brief analogy. My brother once told me that he wanted to write a diet book. His idea was that he would introduce the book with a story like this:

> Bubba drinks soda. For every meal. Breakfast for Bubba? A liter of soda. And none of this "diet" cola. He drinks the real deal. Corn-syrup-infused carbonated bliss in a bottle. Lunch? Exactly the same. Another liter of soda. And for dinner, Bubba has a two-liter bottle of soda. All told, he consumes nothing other than a gallon of soda every day.
>
> Leif follows a different diet. His parents (Moonshadow and Sunlight) taught him the importance of all-natural organic fruits, vegetables, and whole grains. For breakfast, Leif eats stone-ground oats with honey and organic blueberries. For lunch, he eats grilled wild salmon, organic baby asparagus, and a baked sweet potato drizzled with olive oil and fresh herbs. Dinner is spinach salad topped with organic walnuts and balsamic vinegar dressing, quiche made from the eggs of free-range chickens, and a slice of organic wholewheat bread with avocado on it. For dessert, Leif eats a bowl of organic berries in yogurt.
>
> Bubba and Leif follow these exact same diets for an entire month. They exercise equal amounts. The question is: who loses weight?
>
> The obvious answer is Leif. So you know the actual answer must somehow be Bubba.

But why? It's not because Bubba died of diabetes in week one and then lost weight through natural decomposition (though that could certainly happen on an all-soda diet). We're assuming Bubba lived the entire month. So why does he lose weight drinking soda?

It's all about calories in and calories out. Even a gallon of soda adds up to a daily total of only around 1,500 calories. Most Americans burn at least 2,000 calories per day. If Bubba is burning 2,000 calories but only taking in 1,500, he will lose weight. It's simple math.

Leif, on the other hand, is eating at least 2,500 calories, albeit organic ones. So, if he also burns 2,000 calories per day, then he's taking in more than he's burning. That means he'll gain weight. Again, simple math.

It's the same for personal finance. Let's say that both Bubba and Leif make identical salaries of $2,000 per month. They also have identical housing, transportation, taxes, and other expenses of $1,400 per month. But Bubba saves money on groceries. His 30 gallons of soda cost only $100 per month, bringing his total monthly expenses to $1,500. Leif shops at Whole Foods and spends $1,000 per month on groceries. Because his expenses exceed his income, he has to put that on a credit card and (when added to past amounts due) pays another $100 in interest each month. This brings his monthly expenses to $2,500.

The result is that Bubba saves $500 each month, and Leif goes $500 further into debt each month.

This book evaluates personal finance through the lens of mathematics and logic. No, I'm not going to recommend that you move to a diet of all soda to maximize your caloric input per dollar. In fact, when it comes to health-related matters, as well as education and the environment, you're often better off spending money now to save money in the future. We'll get into the details of that later.

What most people need to improve their finances is simple: good information. This book provides concrete, mathematically sound ways to stop spending and start saving and investing in the smartest way possible.

Personal finance and investing are not complicated. It's not a Rube Goldberg structure where you have to make precisely the right choice (investing in this, that, or the other thing) at each juncture to set the next thing in motion to reach your goal.

There are only TWO levers: what comes in and what goes out. Nothing more, nothing less. Make more money than you spend, and your money *will* grow. Think about that. This statement is true even if you are not doing any financial planning. This statement is true even if you do not have a budget. In fact, despite what everyone says, you don't need a budget. All you need to do is make more and spend less.

This book focuses on those two levers and tells you how to pull each as hard as you can. Every chapter provides concrete advice on how to increase your income and decrease your expenses. I've also thrown in some stories to keep you entertained along the way.

The structure of this book is as follows:

Part I: The Goal
Part II: Make More
Part III: Spend Less
Part IV: Invest Wisely

You may notice that Part I (The Goal) contains only four chapters. However, each of those four chapters addresses a weighty and overarching concept. The first chapter explains that the goal of all of this is to reach financial independence so you can retire relatively early if you choose to do so. The second chapter is a reminder that there is a lot more to life than money. The third chapter explains some of the many ways that your financial goals naturally align with protecting the environment. The fourth chapter gives you a simple way to know what to do with extra income.

Part II (Make More) is where you get back every penny you paid for this book and much, much more. This is the really fun part. It has numerous tips for increasing your income today, as well as long-term ways to increase income.

Part III (Spend Less) is full of specific, actionable ways to save money. You'll see that you can implement a lot of these strategies today.

Part IV (Invest Wisely) provides information about stocks and bonds. You'll learn how to figure out where to invest your money to maximize growth while minimizing risk.

Let's get started.

Part I
THE GOAL

1

YOU REALLY CAN RETIRE
(RELATIVELY) EARLY

The best way to understand the two levers (income and expenses) is to plan for your retirement.

If you've just put this book down and cursed my name, I don't blame you. In fact, I'm impressed that you remember my name this early in the book.

Most of us hate thinking about retirement planning. It reminds us of everything we've done wrong.

Take "the miracle of compounding interest." Every time I hear this phrase, I think about how miraculously stupid I am for not saving more before I turned 40. Whenever I read about compound interest, I think, "Great. I'll keep this in mind when I find a time machine."

Just about every book on personal finance reminds its readers of how dumb we all are for not taking advantage of compound interest. They give examples like the following:

Amy starts saving money in high school, putting just $5 into a mutual fund every week. Becky waits until she's 40, and then puts $1,000 per week into a mutual fund. When they both retire at age 65, Amy has $17 billion, and Becky cannot afford to buy a new toaster.

Now if you happen to be reading this book while you're in high school, bravo! Start socking away $5 every week, and you're golden. You won't really get $17 billion, but you'll do quite well.

But for the rest of us, don't worry. Whether you're in your twenties, thirties, forties, fifties, or even if you are already approaching your golden years, it is okay that you never planned for retirement. That describes most of us.

Many of us pour our hearts and souls into our careers. And we're usually quite successful at this. If a career is paying us well, then we assume that money will "work itself out" and we'll have plenty saved by the time we retire.

If, on the other hand, our career is not paying well (even when we're successful), and we are living paycheck-to-paycheck, we are too stressed out about paying bills to even contemplate retirement. This is all okay. In fact, it's to be expected.

But let's change these patterns now. Let's get you on track to what I call FIRRE. This is not a spelling mistake. And it's not about finding your inner tiger. I'll explain the extra "R" in a minute.

If you're not familiar with the FIRE movement, it stands for "financial independence, retire early." The basic concept is to build up a large enough investment portfolio that you can live off it for the rest of your life *without ever needing another paycheck*.

Sounds nice, right? This is the definition of financial independence. As Tanja Hester calls her FIRE-themed (and readworthy) book: *Work Optional*. You can retire early. Or keep working if you want. When you're no longer dependent on a paycheck, the choice is yours.

That's FIRE, and in a moment I'll tell you how you calculate what it will take for you to reach financial independence and retire early. But first I want to tell you about FIRRE: financial independence, retire *relatively* early.

I don't mean relative to your friends and family. When we get into how to lower expenses, you'll learn about why you should *never* compare yourself to others. I'm talking about retiring early relative to when you would retire if you stay on the financial track you're currently on.

You may think you have no chance of retiring before you're eligible for Social Security. Or maybe it's worse and you've already resigned yourself to working until you keel over dead. If that sounds like you, let me say two things. First, welcome to the club. You've just described the vast majority of us. Second, let's see if we can do a little better — keep reading this book and by the end of it, you may see a better path forward.

The 4% Rule

Let's start with the math. A central tenet of the FIRE movement is what is known as the 4% Rule. Some call it the Rule of 25. These concepts are two sides of the same coin.

It's a way to calculate how big a nest egg you need to be financially independent. The idea is that on the day you retire, you can withdraw 4% of your nest egg that year. Every year after that, you take that same number and adjust it upward for inflation, and you can take that new amount from your investments. This is viewed as a safe withdrawal rate, meaning that you can withdraw this amount for at least 30 years, and you will likely never run out of money.

So if you build up a $1 million nest egg, you can withdraw $40,000 in your first year of retirement. Then you can withdraw a larger inflation-adjusted amount each year after that. The hope is that if your investments perform as expected, you will never run out of money.

The Rule of 25 is the same thing but going at it from the other direction. Take your annual expenses and multiply that number by 25 — that's what you need to be financially independent and retire early.

So if you can live off $10,000 a year, you can retire with a $250,000 nest egg. If you need $40,000 per year, then you have to save up $1 million.

And if you have living expenses of $100,000 per year, then you'll need a lot more: $2.5 million to be precise. If that seems undoable, then you may want to skip to Part III of this book, which teaches you how to spend less. Then come back and calculate your new number.

So how do we know the 4% Rule works? We don't. (Nothing is guaranteed.) But there's an enormous amount of research that shows that it does.

Perhaps the best indication that the 4% Rule is onto something is that it has critics on both sides. Some think it is too risky (and thus prefer a 3% or 3.5% withdrawal rate). Others think it is too conservative (and argue that 5% or even as much as 7% is safe).

I like the 4% Rule because it is based on comprehensive studies of long-term market trends. The original research was the Trinity Study. It assumed a balanced portfolio of stocks and bonds. And it took into account worst-case scenarios, such as the Great Depression and other market crashes.

Those studies found that so long as your portfolio contains at least 50% stocks (invested in a low-fee index fund), you can withdraw 4% every year, and you will almost certainly not run out of money. In fact, some of the most recent research shows that when you withdraw 4% every year, there is a 96% chance you'll be left with *more* money than your original starting principal. Your heirs will thank you.

One important note is that the original Trinity Study was based on bond performances that were historically higher than in recent years. Luckily, many people have run updated studies. The more recent studies have led most followers of the 4% Rule to lean toward a higher percentage of stocks (such as 75%), particularly if you are retiring early.

A blogger known as The Poor Swiss recently ran an updated model based on the Trinity Study. He looked at stock and bond performances from 1871 to 2019. His results confirmed that even accounting for inflation, you can withdraw 4% from a portfolio that contains at least 75% stocks, and the portfolio will last at least 30 years nearly every time *(see graph next page)*.

Now it does get a little trickier if you're retiring early and need your portfolio to last longer than 30 years. If that is your plan, and you want to be sure your money lasts at least 50 years, then you may want to go with a 3.5% withdrawal rate. According to The Poor Swiss, a 3.5% withdrawal rate from a portfolio of primarily stocks has an almost 100% chance of succeeding over a 50-year period. And even with a 4% withdrawal rate, the odds are overwhelmingly in your favor that your portfolio will last at least 50 years.

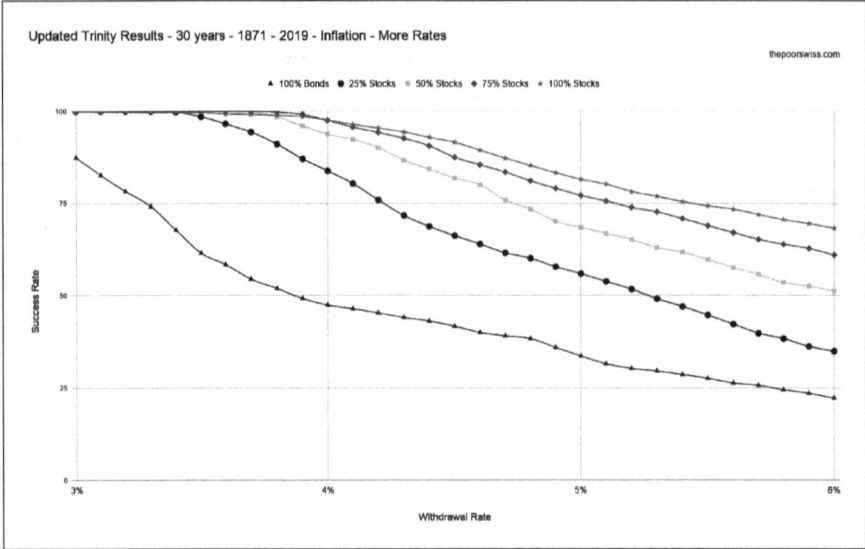

Updated Trinity Results - 30 years - 1871 - 2019 - Inflation - More Rates

thepoorswiss.com

▲ 100% Bonds ● 25% Stocks ▪ 50% Stocks ◆ 75% Stocks ✕ 100% Stocks

One quick note on the above chart: although the 100% stocks portfolio has a higher success rate than a portfolio that includes bonds, you still gain significant benefits from having a portion of your portfolio (for instance, 25%) in bonds. In particular, in the worst-case scenarios where your portfolio fails to survive 4% withdrawals for 30, 40, or 50 years, a mixed portfolio is likely to survive much longer than 100% stocks.

What if the stock market plummets?

If you still are not convinced that the 4% Rule makes sense, let's look at the worst-case scenario and see how it plays out. That scenario is that you retire early and then the next day the stock market plummets. That's really the only time people run into trouble with the 4% Rule. But even that scenario is manageable.

Remember that even after you retire, you still have two levers you can pull at any time. If you retire into a recession, you can pick up part-time work so you do not have to sell stocks when they're at their lowest price. Or you can make minor adjustments to decrease your spending in those early years. By pulling one or both of those levers, you'll do just fine.

How can I possibly save $1 million?

Okay, so let's assume you spend at least $40,000 every year. Now you're wondering how you can possibly ever save $1 million. Do not get discouraged.

There are many paths to retiring relatively early. Even if $1 million (or whatever number you calculated) seems unreachable, remember the thesis of this book: there are always TWO levers you can pull. One is to make more. The other is to spend less. Both levers can be pulled much further than you think.

In one of the most famous articles about FIRE, the blogger Mr. Money Mustache combined the 4% Rule with conservative investment assumptions to show how quickly a high savings rate can lead to financial independence, *regardless of income*. How does this work? If you think about it, your savings rate reflects two things: (1) how much money you're spending, and (2) how much money you're saving and investing. *Note that this assumes that you are investing all the money you don't spend — which you should be doing.*

So if you have a 0% savings rate (meaning you live paycheck-to-paycheck), you'll never achieve financial independence. And if you have a 100% savings rate, you're already financially free, no matter what your income. Of course, if you have a 100% savings rate, then financial freedom is likely the only type of freedom you have since the only way I know of to avoid paying room and board is to be incarcerated.

Where it gets interesting is in the numbers between 0% and 100%. I highly recommend checking out the article *The Shockingly Simple Math Behind Early Retirement* by Mr. Money Mustache.

The short version is that if you only save 10% of your income (the amount that many financial advisors recommend), you have to work for more than 50 years before you reach financial independence. You read that right: 50 years.

On the other hand, if you can get to a 30% savings rate, you can retire in less than 30 years. That extra 20% of savings shaves off more than 20 years from the time it takes you to reach retirement.

And a 50% savings rate gets you to FIRE in just 17 years! Think about that. Yes, it's not easy to save and invest 50% of what you make. But it's also not easy to keep working when you're in your sixties and seventies and want to spend time with your grandchildren or travel the world.

And the possibility of only working for 17 years is mind-boggling. Consider this: if you graduate college at 22, and immediately start saving half of what you earn, you could retire at 39!

If 17 years seems too long to wait, you can drop another decade by saving 75% of your income. At that incredibly high savings rate, financial independence takes just seven years! If even that is too long for you, an 85% savings rate leads to financial independence in only four years.

The easiest way to become a millionaire

Let me also mention the easiest way to become a millionaire. Unfortunately, this strategy is dependent on making regular contributions from an early age. So if (like me) you're already 40 or older and don't have access to a time machine, this strategy is going to be more helpful for your kids.

The easiest way to become a millionaire is to max out your IRA or Roth IRA every year during the course of your career. An IRA is an Individual Retirement Arrangement, although everyone calls them Individual Retirement Accounts. You'll learn lots more about them in Part IV of this book, including the tradeoff between investing in a traditional IRA (which can give you a tax break now) versus a Roth IRA (which allows you to make tax-free withdrawals when you retire). For now, let's just look at what happens when you make regular contributions to either type of account.

Let's say you graduate college at 22 and get your first real job. In 2021, the current maximum IRA contribution for someone under 50 years old is $6,000. That's $500 per month. This might seem like a lot, particularly for a 22-year-old getting their first job. However, as you'll learn later on in this book, most people spend around $9,000 every year for every car they own. If you can find a way to use public transportation, rideshares, biking, and walking, for $3,000 per year ($250 per month), then you have an extra $6,000 to put toward investments each year.

Put another way, if you own a car, you should ask yourself whether you would sell it for a million dollars. As we're about to see, those who invest $6,000 each year can become millionaires by the time they retire.

Here's how it works. If you start investing $500 per month into your IRA or Roth IRA at 22, then all you need to do is continue this for 38 years until you reach age 60. At that point, you can stop making contributions and begin to make withdrawals. (You can actually start at 59 ½, and you can also invest more in an IRA after you turn 50, but we'll ignore those details for now.)

If your investments make a conservative 7% average return over these 38 years, then by the time you turn 60, you'll have $1,035,366. You're a millionaire!

Making more during retirement

Let's go back to how to reach FIRE using our two levers: making more and spending less. Let's start with making more. Remember that the $1 million figure presumes you retire and have no additional income. Any money you bring in during your post-retirement years *drastically* reduces how much you need.

In fact, under the same Rule of 25, every $1,000 (after taxes) of post-retirement income translates to $25,000 less that you need to save for retirement. Every $10,000 of after-tax income reduces the amount you need in your nest egg by $250,000. So if your retirement vision includes part-time consulting or working a few days at your local library, and you know you can make $20,000 per year (after taxes) from that work, you now have $500,000 less to save.

Now is when many people ask, "How is it retirement if I still have to work?" Fair point. But if your new post-retirement job is something you enjoy doing, then why not? There's nothing wrong with planning for semi-retirement, rather than full retirement.

True, you may not be able to kick back at the beach every day and night drinking piña coladas. But you might be able to do exactly that every day if you don't mind tending the bar at night.

Also, you don't have to work to make money. In addition to the money that your investments make for you while you sleep, there are lots of other forms of what is known as *passive* income. This is the "Don't work for money. Make your money work for you!" thing. Passive income is real. Later in this book, we'll talk about how to get it.

In fact, you probably already have at least one form of passive income in the bag: Social Security. It's not entirely guaranteed, since it's currently under-funded, so your benefits might decrease. But most experts say that Social Security will still be there when you need it. If you don't plan to retire until 67, and Social Security will provide you $20,000 per year, then you no longer need a $1 million nest egg to have $40,000 in income. You only need $500,000. With-drawing 4% of $500,000 will give you $20,000. Add that to your $20,000 from Social Security, and you have the $40,000 you need.

And Social Security is not the only passive income out there. For instance, anyone who has worked for local, state, or federal government (including the military) will likely have a pension. If this work was only for part of your career, then it may not be a big pension, but even a small pension can drastically reduce the amount of money you need for your nest egg.

Granted, the math gets more complicated if you want to retire early before you have access to Social Security (and maybe also a pension). But it's not that complicated. You just need to do two calculations. First, figure out how much you need at the time that Social Security and any pension kick in. This will be a much smaller number than what you need to be financially independent with-out Social Security or a pension. Second, figure out how much you need in the preceding years. This number will also be smaller than what you would need to be financially independent under the 4% Rule. That's because you can count on withdrawing more than 4% during these years when you know that you won't need as much money when you get Social Security.

In addition to Social Security and pensions, there are lots of other forms of passive income that keep paying even after you retire. Rental real estate is a big one. Someone who owns a few multi-unit rentals may be able to bring in $20,000 in cash flow every year. Adding that to Social Security, they might not need any nest egg at all! Or, better yet, they could still build a nest egg and use it to retire before 67.

Stock dividends are another form of passive income, although you cannot double-count here if these are part of the portfolio you're using when you calcu-late the 4% Rule. The 4% Rule presumes you are reinvesting all dividends.

Other potential passive income sources include royalties from intellectual property like books, music, and patents. Those royalties can help fund your post-retirement years.

Spending less during retirement

Let's now turn to the other lever: expenses. Your annual expenses are far more flexible than you think. And here is a crucial point: decreasing your expenses today performs *double duty*. It lowers the amount you need in your nest egg because you have learned to live on less. It also increases your savings rate (the amount you can invest), which brings you closer every day to having what you need to retire.

For instance, if you currently pay $100 per month for cable, you have to save an extra $30,000 (the annual expense of $1,200 multiplied by 25) to retire! Now here's where the double duty comes in. If you eliminate that $100 bill and instead invest $100 every month for the next 15 years, then, even at just a 7% interest rate, you'll have over $30,000. That means this one change — getting rid of cable — brought you $60,000 closer to retirement!

Another place you can find huge savings is by paying off your mortgage before you retire. If you can live off $40,000 a year now, and $15,000 of that annual expense is for your mortgage, that means you can actually live off $25,000 a year. And let's say you and your partner have two cars now, but you know you'll be able to move to one car when you retire, saving you at least another $5,000 per year in car payments, insurance, and maintenance costs. With these two changes, your living expenses have been cut in half, and your FIRE number just went from $1 million to $500,000.

This is probably the best-kept secret of the FIRE movement. The vast majority of 30- and 40-somethings who have already retired early did so not by making more money, but by spending less.

This brings me to one final point: ignore any retirement calculator that is based on a percentage of your income. Many people claim that you need "at least 85%" of your income to survive retirement. Really? So if a Fortune 500 CEO is making $20 million a year, there is no way she can retire until she has set aside enough money to cover $17 million in annual expenses? You know, I have a feeling that she could probably make ends meet on $16 million a year.

Let me be clear: there is *no* correlation between your income and what you need for retirement. As J.D. Roth from *Get Rich Slowly* explains, basing your retirement needs on your current income is "like trying to guess how much fuel you'll use on a trip to grandmother's house based on the size of your vehicle's gas tank!"

Your retirement needs should not be a function of your income. If one person makes $30,000 a year and another person makes $100,000 a year, but they have both learned to live on $20,000 in annual expenses, then they both need the same sized nest egg to retire. Sure, the person making $100,000 a year will find it much easier to save up that money. But my point is that the actual amount of money needed is identical.

It's complete hogwash that you need to have 85% (or any other percentage) of your income in retirement. So where did this myth come from? It comes from the dangerous assumption that, in a consumer-driven society, everyone will increase their spending as they increase their income.

Sadly, this is often exactly what happens. When I told my dad that I was writing a book on personal finance (and gave him a heads-up that he'd be featured in it), he mentioned that he and my mom were going to be cleaning the house that weekend "because an appraiser is coming."

"Dad, you know it's better not to clean your house when the town lister comes," I said. "You want it to look bad so your property taxes stay low."

"No, it's not for property taxes," he said. "We're refinancing the home."

"Is this to get out of that balloon mortgage you signed up for? That makes sense. With the rates so low, we're also looking into 15-year mortgages now."

"We can't afford to do a 15-year," my dad said. "We're going to have to get a 30-year."

I couldn't believe what my dad had just said. He's 76 years old! And he's getting a 30-year mortgage?

When I mentioned the low 2.75% rate our local bank was offering for 15-year mortgages, he said that "at that rate, maybe the 15-year would be doable."

I couldn't help but add the following response: "Yes, and you'd have the added benefit of not having to still make payments when you're 106."

That conversation actually happened. I should add that this is the home I grew up in. My parents bought it 35 years ago. They've made payments on it for 35 years. But they've refinanced it so many times that they still have another 30 years of payments to go. This is why so many people, including my parents, can never retire, even though their incomes are above average.

This is where I'm counting on you to be different. We're all guilty of spending more as our income has increased. I've certainly done it many times. But this pattern can change.

2

THERE IS A LOT MORE
TO LIFE THAN MONEY

B efore we jump into the details of *how* to make more money and spend less, it's important to think about *why* we want financial independence. There are many reasons to pursue financial independence. They can be as simple as "My boss is mean and I never want to work again." That is as good a reason as any. But there are lots of other reasons as well.

Let me tell you something really important (which I suspect you already know): money is a means, not an end. When we talk about financial independence and retiring early, we're not actually talking about money. We're talking about time. Our time. A limited resource that can never be replaced.

If you have not yet read *Your Money or Your Life*, by Vicki Robin and Joe Dominguez, you should make sure you do so. While everyone understands at some level that time is money and money is time, *Your Money or Your Life* explains this concept in much greater detail. It's truly eye-opening to learn how much of your life ends up being spent doing work for other people just to make money.

How you spend your time matters far more than how you spend your money. But money is often a prerequisite to being able to spend your time as you wish. If, for instance, you want to be with your kids during their childhood, or be able to travel the world — on your own or with your family in later years — you'll need money. Just remember that it's time, not money, that we're really chasing.

Also, there is nothing selfish about taking care of your financial situation. In fact, if you have a partner or a family, this is one of the biggest gifts you can ever give them.

Parents often spend a lot on their children — sports, music lessons, books, and education. I know my partner and I are guilty of this. When we buy things for our kids, we feel good about it, and we view these as necessary expenses.

Saving for retirement, on the other hand, feels like more of a selfish endeavor. It's not. If you have a family, then saving for retirement is for them far more than it's for you. After all, these are the people who will end up paying for you in old age if you haven't planned ahead. Do them a favor and start moving toward financial independence now.

I know my main reason for seeking financial independence is to have more time with my family and less time with my stress. Like most people, I never get enough time with my partner, my three kids, my friends, or myself. As for my stress, on the other hand, that gets lots of my time.

Over the course of my life, two of the biggest sources of stress have always been my job (I mentioned that I'm a lawyer, right?) and, more generally, finances. Watching a bank account creep lower and lower every day, and not knowing if you'll have enough to pay your bills or put food on the table, is incredibly stressful — on both you and your loved ones. Money is stressful because you need it to pay for shelter and to feed your family.

Financial stress is a leading cause of marital discord. If you have a partner, then you have almost certainly had fights over finances.

And here's another key point: you need money to avoid losing money. It's no secret that banks, credit card companies, and other money lenders are not charitable organizations. They're profiteers, and they prey on poor people. Rich people are not paying bank overdraft fees or a 20% annual percentage rate on unpaid credit card bills. They are not paying private mortgage insurance to own a house, and they never pay late fees either. It's those who can least afford these expenses that always end up paying them.

Your journey toward financial independence will improve your financial situation immensely, regardless of whether you ever reach the final goal. If you are currently living paycheck-to-paycheck, then, like I said before, welcome to the club. That's the vast majority of us. It's what most of my adult life has been. And it's tough. When you are struggling to meet daily expenses, it is hard to give any serious thought to retirement. Financial independence probably sounds like a pipe dream. But if you try for it anyway, your life will be far better for it.

So, let's dig into this idea of financial independence. What does that mean anyway? This is what many refer to as financial freedom. That is the key. Not money. As I mentioned, money is (by definition) a means, not an end. It's freedom — life — that you get when you reach financial independence.

Your time is worth far more than money will ever be. And when you reach financial freedom, you get to choose how to spend your time. Once you have saved up enough money to live off it, you really are free. You've exited the rat race. Because you do not have to show up for work at nine every morning, the options are limitless.

Spend some time thinking about what your life might look like when you no longer need to work. This is very personal. I can't tell you how to spend your time once you are financially free.

I will, however, make two suggestions: give your time and your money, and prioritize education and experiences over consumption.

Give your time and money

The ability to give your time and money freely is one of the biggest benefits of financial independence. If that does not motivate you to seek financial independence, then I do not know what will.

And here's a crucial point about giving your time and money: you can do this not just when you retire, but also while you are on your financial journey. This seems counterintuitive, but stick with me and I'll explain.

Most personal finance books focus entirely on precisely that — personal finances. These books tell you how you, personally, can save money to get out of debt or retire comfortably. In fact, as you'll see, the bulk of this book does the same thing. But no one is an island. Humans are social creatures, and we are deeply interconnected and interdependent.

No, I'm not going to start preaching about taking care of your neighbors. (Okay, I might preach a little bit.) All I'm saying is that taking care of your finances is not — and should not — be a selfish pursuit. Far from it. When you get your financial house in order, you have more bandwidth to help friends, family, and charitable causes. And you can start doing this now.

By practicing giving your time and money now, you'll find out why financial independence is so important. You'll realize that if you make more and spend less, you'll be able to give much more than you ever have before, and you'll be that much closer to financial independence.

It is often our investments in people — those we care the most about — that pay the biggest dividends. You cannot put a price tag on the phone call or text you get from your best friend when you're having a bad day. Or on the sibling who reaches out to make sure you're okay when disaster strikes. These social ties are more valuable than any money you'll ever save.

This does not mean you should go crazy and give all your money to anyone who asks for it. Again, you'll be able to give far more money and time later if you make prudent choices today. So, for instance (and at the risk of offending people by saying this), if you are involved in a religious practice, consider whether you really should pay a full 10% tithe at this time in your life. Maybe something more modest makes sense for now while you're investing, and maybe that will free you up to pay much more later.

In fact, by investing more now, you will be able to make far larger donations to charitable causes when you retire. This is so for two reasons. First, your investment will grow over time, taking advantage of compound interest. Second, when you use investment funds for charitable donations, you can make much larger contributions by taking advantage of tax benefits.

Let me explain this second point. After recent changes to tax law, nearly all filers now use the standard deduction, rather than itemized deductions. If you use the standard deduction, then your charitable donations are made with after-tax dollars. This means that if you have $10,000 in extra income, and you pay 15% in taxes, then you can only donate $8,500. You'll need to save the other $1,500 to pay taxes. If, however, you wait until you can use investment proceeds for donations, then, with advice from a tax planner, you may be able to donate the full $10,000 and not owe the government anything.

There are a few ways to do this. For instance, you may be able to donate stock sales and have your chosen charity receive the full $10,000, even though you would have received only $8,500 after taxes if you took the money and then donated. And if you're 72 or older and have to start paying taxes on mandatory withdrawals from an IRA, you can use Qualified Charitable Deductions for significant tax advantages. Again, instead of paying $8,500 to your charity and $1,500 to the government, your charity could get the whole $10,000.

But let me be clear: I'm not advising you to be miserly. Remember this chapter is about how there is much more to life than money. I'm just saying that, as with all financial decisions, you should put some thought and planning into how and when you give.

Be selective about how you spend your time and where you spend and save money. Do not stop going out with friends just because it costs too much money. You may want to think about how to save money by changing the setting (for instance, potlucks rather than dining at restaurants and bars). But do not become a hermit. And do not be miserly. If you end up at a restaurant or bar with friends, be the person who pays more than their fair share of the bill.

Prioritize education and experiences over consumption

Lots of personal finance books tell you to save money everywhere and on everything. I disagree. You always want to look for ways to save money on consumer goods, but I don't recommend scrimping when it comes to education and experiences.

Education and experiences pay dividends forever. Whether it's classes, books, traveling, museums, social gatherings, live sports events, concerts, or anything else. Memorable experiences are worth their weight in gold.

The consumption of material goods, on the other hand, does not pay dividends. It just drains your bank account. And, sorry to make things grim, but when you're on your deathbed, you won't remember what you bought. You'll remember what you did and the people you did it with.

While education and experiences usually cost money, they tend to increase your ability to make money. Often by a lot. Whatever your profession, the education you've had, combined with all of your life experiences, will make you better at your job. As a result, you will earn more money.

A single $10 or $15 book can change your life. For instance (and this is just a randomly selected example), this book. After you finish reading this book, you will be making more and spending less. This will hopefully be the best investment you've ever made.

And if you really want to save on expenses, keep in mind that lots of education and experiences are free. My entire college degree was on a full scholarship. (They even paid for my books!) And my partner and I have seen some of the most amazing live performances imaginable for free. See more on this in my chapter on "Get ENTERTAINED for Free." In fact, the way we saw some of those events (offering to usher for them) at times led to an even richer experience than we would have had if we had paid for them. Like standing a foot away from Bobby McFerrin while he does a call-and-response with your father-in-law.

But we also happily pay for these experiences. Ramit Sethi (the author of *I Will Teach You to Be Rich*) has a great saying: "spend extravagantly on the things you love, and cut costs mercilessly on the things you don't." I agree. For me, education and experiences are things that I love. They are always worth the cost.

3

GREEN MAKES GREEN

When I was in high school, I got up early one morning and saw my dad pulling his car into our driveway. Not leaving, but arriving. This was odd, to say the least, given that it was only six in the morning.

"Where'd you go, Dad?" I asked.

"To get my iced tea," he said, holding up a plastic Big Gulp sized cup that was still half full.

"You drove to get iced tea?"

"Yeah, I go every morning."

As we talked more, my dad mentioned the gas station he went to every morning, where they sold his enormous cup of iced tea for only 99 cents.

What my dad failed to consider was that this gas station was over 20 miles away! That means he was driving more than 40 miles each morning. To get a cup of iced tea.

Let's quickly break this down from two perspectives: a green one and another green one. First, let's consider the financial impact of driving 40 miles every day to get a cup of tea. Then we'll consider the environmental impacts.

From a purely financial standpoint, driving 40 miles costs at least $10 and arguably as much as $24. According to the IRS, each mile of driving costs nearly 60 cents. By this calculation, my dad was spending around $24 every morning to get a cup of tea.

However, that's probably too high a number, as it includes a portion of all of the fixed (or sunk) costs of car ownership (like monthly payments, insurance, registration, and other costs that he has to pay regardless of how much he drives). Of course, if he didn't leave the house before dawn every morning to buy a cup of iced tea, or make all the other unnecessary trips he makes the rest of the day, he could probably share a car with my mom, and they would save all of those costs. From that perspective, the $24 estimate may be quite accurate for 40 miles of unnecessary driving.

But let's give my dad the benefit of the doubt and look only at marginal costs (how much it costs to drive an extra 40 miles in a car you already own). These are still significant. In 2021, with gas prices between two and three dollars per gallon, the marginal costs add up to around 25 cents per mile (10 cents per mile in gas, 10 cents toward maintenance, and 5 cents in depreciation because higher-mileage cars sell for less). That means he's paying $10 every morning for his cup of iced tea — before he even pays for it!

In other words, his "99 cent" cup of iced tea actually costs $11 and arguably as much as $25. Every day! Even using the lower figure of $11, this means he's paying over $4,000 per year for iced tea!

Now let's talk about the other green perspective. How much does my dad's iced-tea habit contribute to climate change? More than you'd think. These 40 miles of completely unnecessary driving have a significant carbon footprint, particularly because it's a daily routine.

My dad's car gets decent mileage, but it's not great. We live in Vermont, so he has all-wheel drive. This means that his sedan gets around 22 miles to the gallon. So a 40-mile drive wastes nearly two gallons of gas. That's around 15,000 grams of carbon dioxide entering the atmosphere each day, just so my dad can have his cup of iced tea. That's over five million grams of carbon dioxide every year.

My dad is of course oblivious to all of this. If he knew he was spending $4,000 per year on iced tea, he might think twice about it. And he'd also think twice if he knew that this same habit was pumping five million grams of carbon dioxide into the atmosphere every year.

The environment provides another compelling reason to change your habits now so that you make more and spend less. (I told you I might preach a little bit, right?)

The fact is that we are far beyond the point where environmentalism is a "luxury." Clean air, clean water, and a livable climate are not luxuries. There is no point in saving a $1 million nest egg for retirement if the nest holding your egg has burned up in flames.

Many of the chapters in this book suggest ways to make more or spend less that (if followed) will also benefit the environment. But the environment also deserves its own chapter in this book because every financial decision we make has environmental consequences. And we are at a moment in time like no other. We can no longer take our precious Earth for granted. The environment needs to be front and center in every decision humans make.

Okay, enough preaching. Now let's turn to practical advice.

There are lots of books about how to lower your carbon footprint or make other choices to help the environment. Those books rarely address the impact of those choices on your finances. Some books do address this overlap, but unfortunately gloss over which lifestyle changes actually save money and which ones cost more.

This book provides concrete ways to save your bank account and the environment. This is how you do well by doing good.

Let me give one quick example of how you can save enormous amounts of money and carbon emissions: downsizing your home.

Your home is likely your biggest monthly expense. This is true whether you rent or own. And it's true even if you've already paid off your entire mortgage. Between property taxes, insurance, repairs, heating, cooling, utilities, and cleaning, you're paying a lot to have a roof over your head. And the bigger the shelter, the more you pay.

Downsizing is the biggest change you can make right now to decrease your monthly expenses and bring you closer to retirement. Downsizing not only drastically reduces your monthly expenses but also lowers your carbon footprint. Big time.

If you want to reach financial independence and retire early, you should think about downsizing your home.

Even better: look into "house hacking." House hacking, in a nutshell, is buying a house that has multiple units (or at least multiple bedrooms) and living in one unit while renting out all of the extra units or bedrooms. This is one of the best ways to not only save money but make money.

Not that long ago, it was quite common for many adults to share a living space, even after college. My mom did this when she lived in Vermont in the early 1970s before she met my dad. She shared a house with seven other people. This worked out well and saved her tons of money on rent at the time. The only downside was that when she started dating my dad, he would occasionally embarrass her when he did things like show up at her house dressed in a maroon one-piece jumpsuit.

House hacking simultaneously pulls on both levers — reducing expenses and increasing income. If you do it right, you can get the rental income to not only cover your mortgage, property taxes, repairs, and all other expenses but also provide you with additional cash flow. Pretty neat, huh?

Can you imagine having an extra $1,000 or $2,000 added to your bank account every month? No other lifestyle change can give you that big a boost in your savings. (Unless you literally burn money to start fires, in which case you should start using paper — that will save you lots more money.)

House hacking has played a crucial role in many members of the current FIRE generation who have achieved financial independence in their 30s or 40s. If you can find a way to live without paying rent or mortgage, do it. If you can make a profit from your housing, even better.

There are lots of good books and other resources on house hacking, including the BiggerPockets website, podcasts, books, and social media groups. An excellent book for learning more about house hacking — and other ways to accelerate your path to financial independence — is *Set for Life*, by BiggerPockets CEO Scott Trench.

But what if you're stuck paying rent or a mortgage? Most of us are. For this group, you'll want to do anything and everything to minimize those expenses. The best way to simultaneously reduce every home-related living expense is to downsize.

Consider the following graph. These expenses are hypothetical, but they approximate what two people might spend on each of the housing-related items that are listed:

MONTHLY EXPENSE	FRUGAL FRED (700 SQUARE FOOT APARTMENT)	SPENDY SAM (5,000 SQUARE FOOT HOUSE)
Mortgage	$700	$5,000
Property Taxes	$200	$1,000
Heating & Cooling	$200	$800
Utilities	$200	$600
Homeowners' Insurance	$100	$300
Repairs	$100	$300
TOTAL	**$1,500 per month**	**$8,000 per month**

That's a difference of $6,500 per month, which is $78,000 per year. This does not even account for other expenses that are often incurred when you own an enormous home (like hiring cleaning professionals). Granted, this is an extreme example — most families fall somewhere in between $1,500 per month and $8,000 per month in housing expenses. But it illustrates how much money downsizing can save.

And you're not just saving your wallet when you downsize. You're saving the planet as well. In general, the smaller your house, the smaller your carbon footprint. Look at the items in the chart above that are carbon-intensive: heating and cooling, and utilities. Frugal Fred saves $1,000 per month on those items alone. That's $1,000 that Frugal Fred can save, invest, or spend on things that emit less carbon.

If everyone downsized their homes today, that would probably move us closer to addressing climate change than any other action individuals can take.

This is an area where modern-day Americans have fallen behind everyone else in the world, as well as previous generations of Americans. In other words, we have fallen behind everyone who is alive today and everyone who has ever lived. The rest of the world knows that you don't need 1,000 square feet per person.

When our third child was born, our family of five and our large golden retriever all lived in an apartment that was less than 700 square feet. Granted, that was pretty cramped, so we soon bought a house.

But we didn't get a big house. We moved into a place that is 1,400 square feet. It's tight, but it works. And it's luxurious compared to the living situations in most parts of the world.

Downsizing your home is not the only way that green makes green. Throughout the rest of this book, you'll find lots of other ways that being green improves your finances.

4

WHAT TO DO WITH EXTRA MONEY: ONE SPREADSHEET TO RULE THEM ALL

O kay, we're about to dive into the details of how to make more and spend less. In the upcoming chapters, I'm going to provide you with concrete steps that will increase your income and decrease your expenses. But before we do that, let's talk a little about what to do with the piles of extra money you'll soon have.

It turns out that there's a very simple way to figure out where to put your extra money. Here's what to do. First, get out a sheet of paper and a pen. Or hop into a spreadsheet if you're a spreadsheet geek — you know who you are! Then make a list of every investment you have and every debt you have.

Now add in the interest rate for each investment and debt, and order the list from the highest interest rate to the lowest. It doesn't matter if the interest rate is what you make on your investments or what you pay for your debts. All that matters is the number itself. *This is the most important part: your list must be in order from highest interest rate to lowest.*

Note that for your investments, you may have to make educated guesses based on anticipated returns. And if you do not currently have any investments, put in placeholders for the investments you intend to make.

Here is an example of what your list might look like (with debts in italics and assets in bold):

Jane Doe's One Spreadsheet to Rule Them All

Investment or Debt	Amount	Interest Rate
Matched Portion of 401(k)	**$3,000 per year**	**+ 105%**
Visa Card	$2,500	- 22%
American Express Card	$1,500	- 20%
Vanguard Index Fund	**$5,000**	**+ 9%**
Federal Student Loans	$230,000	- 7.9%
PAX World Roth IRA	**$35,000**	**+ 7%**
Private Student Loans	$30,000	- 6.5%
Jane's Used Car Loan	$5,000	- 6%
Unmatched Portion of 401(k)	**$10,000**	**+ 5%**
Joe's Used Car Loan	$11,000	- 3%
Mortgage	$140,000	- 2.75%
High-Yield Savings Account	**$1,000**	**+ 1.1%**
Regular Savings Account	**$300**	**+ 0.1%**
Checking Account	**$1,500**	**+ 0.0%**
Bag Hidden Under Mattress	**$1,000**	**+ 0.0%**

This, my friend, is your list of priorities. Well, this is Jane's list. You'll need to make your own.

Then all you need to do is start at the top and work your way down.

If the first item on your list is an investment, then additional money would be used first to fund that investment. So, for instance, Jane's top priority should be to fully fund the matched portion of her 401(k). Her anticipated return for that investment is 103% because she would get an immediate return of 100% from her employer's match, followed by an anticipated return of 3% from the investment. This 103% interest rate is far higher than any of the other interest rates for any of her other investments and debts.

If the first item on your list is a debt, then you would prioritize paying off that debt whenever you have additional money. You would put additional money toward paying off that debt in its entirety before you would move on to sending more money to any of your other debts or investments.

Of course, for all of your debts, you'll have to make the minimum payments. But once you've covered all of your minimum payments, any extra money should focus on the top of the list, and, in general, you should make additional payments in that order.

Keep in mind that payments on debt offer you a *guaranteed* rate of return. If the rate of return on your investments is not guaranteed, then you would be wise to prioritize paying off debt if the interest on that debt is close to what you expect from your investment. It's obvious that you should pay down your used car loan when it costs you 6%, rather than getting an estimated 5% return in the unmatched portion of your 401(k). But you may also want to prioritize paying off your 6% used car loan even if you expect your Pax World Roth IRA to make an average return of 7%. The 6% you save on debt is guaranteed, while your investment gains are always only estimates.

Note that you should only favor paying off debt if the numbers are really close (for instance, as in the above example, within 1%). If your Vanguard account is expected to make 9%, then you would want to put more money in that before you pay down your 2.75% mortgage.

One more caveat: some of your debt may have benefits that make it worth holding on to for longer than you might otherwise. For instance, student loan debt carries certain advantages. If you have any chance of qualifying for federal student loan forgiveness, your best bet may be to make only minimum payments on those loans. (Much more on this later.) Also, the interest you pay on federal and private student loans provides you with a significant tax benefit. You can currently deduct up to $2,500 in interest on student loans every year, and this deduction is in addition to your standard deduction. So you may want to prioritize paying other debts first.

Make sure you alter your spreadsheet whenever you get a new asset or debt, and whenever an interest rate changes. And take a good look at those interest rates on a regular basis with these two questions in mind: (1) for my assets, is there any way to increase the interest rate? (2) for my debts, is there any way to decrease the interest rate?

By the time you get to the end of this book, you should have a few answers to both of those questions. For instance, Jane is paying way too high an interest rate for private student loans. If she has good credit, refinancing could bring that 6.5% rate down to more like 4%.

Jane also has $4,000 in credit card debt, all at 20% interest or higher. That should be paid off immediately.

But if Jane does not have any extra money coming in, she may need to find a more creative way to pay off this debt. One option would be to cash out her $1,000 high-yield savings account and grab the $1,000 under her bed, but that still leaves her short $2,000. Where can she find another $2,000?

Although there are many options out there (like a personal loan or a debt consolidation loan), let me offer one that most people don't know about: refinancing your car.

Did you know that cars can be refinanced to provide you with cash in hand? I know that came as a surprise to me. If you bought your car a few years ago, can you really take out another loan on it and get a check from the bank? Yes. So long as the car's Blue Book value is more than what you owe, and you have good credit, you can use the equity in your car to get a very low-interest loan.

Note that Jane's car loan for Joe's used car is at a low 3% interest. This is not hypothetical — my family currently has a 2.99% six-year car loan that we got from our credit union.

You're probably not going to find a better rate on a car loan than 3%, because 3% is awfully good. In fact, when you look at the spreadsheet, you can see that the 3% car loan is a much better rate than what Jane is paying on all her other debt, except her mortgage.

Jane could check with a credit union or bank about refinancing her car at the same rate for $13,000 (rather than the $11,000 owed now), and then use the extra $2,000 the bank gives her, combined with her other money, to wipe out her credit card debt for good. With enough equity in the new car, Jane could take out an even larger 3% loan and use the additional cash to pay off the entirety of the 6% loan on her other car. Yes, this increases the payments owed on the remaining car loan, but it saves hundreds of dollars in interest.

Another way to think about your spreadsheet is that you want to lower the dollar value and interest rate on any debts, and you want to increase the dollar value and interest rate of your investments. And anytime you can get rid of top-line debt items, do it.

In general, assets should make at least 5% in interest and debts should be below 5%.

Keep your spreadsheet handy and stick to it. This is the math way of doing personal finance.

Part II
MAKE MORE

5

FREE MONEY EXISTS

One day while I was in high school, I came home and found my dad in the basement surrounded by a thousand envelopes, a stack of a thousand letters, and sheets and sheets of address labels.

"What are you doing, Dad?" I asked.

"Here, take a look," he said and showed me a letter he had received in the mail. The letter had contained a one-dollar bill and explained that my dad would make thousands of dollars if he simply reprinted this letter and sent it, along with five address labels, to a thousand other people.

The idea was that each of those thousand people would do the same, eventually reaching hundreds of thousands of people. The five address labels were for the four previous senders in the chain, along with my dad. And the instructions in each letter said to send a $1 bill to each of those five people. My dad diligently sent out a $1 bill to each of the five people on the list he received.

If you're confused by now, that's because none of this makes any sense. It was an idiotic chain-letter scam.

A ten-second Google search revealed that *every* single one of these chain letters originated from an address labeling company. Surely the same company that my dad sent $500 to as he embarked on this get-rich-quick scheme. He also spent another $500 or so on the envelopes and stamps, and then paid me around $100 for helping him put the mailings together.

So all told he was in for over a grand. But boy was it exciting over the next few months when not one, not two, but *three* whole dollars arrived by mail!

This chapter, titled "FREE Money Exists," is *not* about get-rich-quick schemes. I don't have any secrets that will make you an overnight millionaire. No one does. But I do have some tips for how to make a few hundred, or even a few thousand, dollars with very little effort. I've done most of these myself, and they work. If you make it no further than the end of this chapter, you will have made back more money than whatever you spent buying this book.

Free Money Tip #1:
Max out your employer's 401(k) match

You nailed the interview. Your new employer calls you up and says (no surprise) they want to hire you. Then the salary negotiation begins, and it goes like this:

"We can pay you $50,000," they say.

You're smart, you did your research, and you know they can do a little better.

"I really need $53,000," you say. "If you can make it $53,000, I'll be there in two weeks."

"That's more than we were planning on," they reply. "But we'll make it work — $53,000 it is."

"Thanks," you tell them.

Then you add, "but I was just kidding. I only want $50,000. You can keep the other $3,000."

In real life, no one would ever say that. Yet that is, in effect, happening every day all across the country. Millions of Americans fail to contribute to their 401(k) or a similar employer-sponsored plan even though their employer would match those contributions.

For instance, let's say an employer offers a 100% match up to 6% of an employee's salary. Many employers offer that exact match program. If the employee then chooses *not* to put any money into her 401(k), she is choosing to be paid $50,000 a year, rather than $53,000.

You should contact your employer today and find out if they offer a 401(k) or another retirement plan. These plans go by many names, and each works slightly differently. Some other names for employer-sponsored plans are Roth 401(k), 403(b), 457, Savings Incentive Match Plan for Employees (SIMPLE) IRA, Simplified Employee Pension (SEP) IRA, and Thrift Savings Plan.

If your employer offers a retirement plan, then find out whether they match contributions. If they do, find out exactly how much is matched, and make sure you maximize the employer's match.

Note that many employers offer only a 50% match, rather than a 100% match. No problem. It's still free money. Get every penny of it.

You will likely need to choose a particular fund to invest this money in. Don't sweat it. This is not the time for analysis paralysis. You can close your eyes and select *any* investment plan at random and you will have just made the best investment of your life. That's because, no matter what you picked, you already doubled your money (a 100% rate of return) right off the bat.

Better yet, do a little research. Find out if your employer offers a Roth 401(k) or any other type of Roth option, as these can provide significant tax benefits. (See my later chapter on "TAXES Are Not Inevitable.") And make sure you look for broad-based index funds that have the lowest fees. As you'll learn in Part IV of this book ("Invest Wisely"), low-fee index funds are often the best bet.

Free Money Tip #2:
Get a bonus for opening a new checking account

This actually works. You need to read the fine print, and you need to pay attention to make sure you don't pick up any fees. But you really can get free money just for opening a new checking account.

I've done this twice in the last year or so. One bank offered a $600 bonus for opening a new account and setting up a direct deposit of at least $2,000 in one month. I got the $600. Then I closed the account.

A few months later, I did a Google search for similar bonuses. I learned that another bank offered a 3% cash bonus for all direct deposits during a six-month period, up to $700. After reading the fine print and learning that I could make large enough direct deposits to avoid any fees for this account, I signed up. The way the timing worked out for my first direct deposit, I missed out on $20 of this bonus, but I successfully received the other $680!

In one year, I made $1,280 just like that.

Free Money Tip #3:
Get a bonus for opening a new savings account

Banks also offer bonuses for opening savings accounts. These tend to be less accessible to the average person because they usually require a minimum deposit of $10,000 or more, so this is not something I've ever tried. But if you have a big pile of cash sitting in your savings account, look into whether you would qualify for one of these bonuses. You might be able to make hundreds of dollars simply by moving your money around every few months. You do want to make sure that wherever you put your money is FDIC insured.

Free Money Tip #4:
Open a high-yield savings account

Speaking of cash hanging out in a savings account, how's that working out for you? I logged into my savings account the other day and noticed "activity" reflecting a few pennies added last month in interest. Literally a few pennies. Again, a quick Google search showed me that I could open an online high-yield savings account and get a much better rate. The same bank where I opened my new checking account offered over 1% interest in high-yield savings. Done. As soon as my direct deposits hit the new checking account (where they get a 3% bonus), I can log in and transfer that money to high-yield savings. Now I just gave myself a 4% raise!

Free Money Tip #5:
Get a bonus for opening a new credit card

Credit cards also offer excellent sign-up bonuses. Here's where I need to offer a big disclaimer: as you already know, do not ever get, or use, a credit card unless you can (and will) pay the full balance of the card every single month. Just one month of interest, let alone years of it, can easily wipe out any benefit you get from a sign-up bonus.

And don't buy more things just to make your minimum spend to get a sign-up bonus. That also cancels out any of the benefits a sign-up bonus provides.

If you're following those rules, and you have a good enough credit score to qualify for new cards, you should look into getting a big sign-up bonus for your new card. I've made anywhere from $150 to $500 just for signing up and making a minimum spend on things I was going to buy anyway. The $500 deals are rare, but they're out there — just keep an eye out for them.

Lots of people recommend using credit cards to rack up frequent flyer miles for "travel hacking." They look for sign-up bonuses that offer 20,000 or even as much as 80,000 miles. If you know you're going to buy lots of plane tickets next year, then go for it. You get more bang for the buck when you use miles for plane tickets you would have bought otherwise.

But keep in mind that frequent flyer miles are not the same as cash. You're often limited to one airline. Or your miles are "universal" and treated as cash so long as you purchase your plane tickets through a particular website. The only problem is that those websites often charge more than what you'd pay on Travelocity, Expedia, Orbitz, or Kayak. And if you end up not using your miles, they often expire. In other words, the payback is a lot less certain.

That's why I always prefer straight-up cash bonuses.

Free Money Tip #6:
Get cash back on a credit card

In addition to sign-up bonuses, lots of credit cards offer cash back. Again, this is free money. You just use your card as you normally would and then every few months you click a few buttons online, and the amount due is suddenly a few hundred dollars less. I've made thousands of dollars in free money since I discovered and started using cash-back cards.

My favorite card is the American Express Blue Cash Preferred. In 2021, it costs $95 every year, but you get 6% cash back for the first $6,000 you spend on groceries. This benefit alone equates to $360 if (like my family) you always spend at least $500 a month on groceries. So just looking at cash back from groceries, we net $265 every year we have this card. Adding in 3% cash back for gas and 1% on everything else, and we always make over $300 in free money every year.

I also recently discovered a Visa card from Alliant Bank that provides 2.5% cash back for every purchase, with a promotional rate of 3% cash back on all purchases during the first year. The annual fee for this card is waived in the first year, but after that, it currently costs $99 per year, so we'll have to see how much we use it to determine if 2.5% cash back is worth $99 per year. (It may be that we'd do better with a 2% cash-back card that does not carry an annual fee.) We're currently using this card for everything except groceries and gas.

Again, Google is your friend here. Search for cash-back credit cards and with a little bit of research, you can find the one that will maximize your free money.

Free Money Tip #7: Get cash back for online purchases

I've never been a coupon clipper, and I never will be. The problem with coupons is that they require me to spend time that I'd rather spend doing other things. But, as you know, the internet is changing everything.

A couple of years ago, I created an online account with Ebates, which is now called Rakuten. I downloaded an extension in my web browser. Note that this undoubtedly means that Rakuten is tracking all of my online shopping, but I figure that my browser is already doing that anyway. For me, the convenience is worth it. Now, whenever I'm about to buy something online, I first click the Rakuten button on my browser, and, for the vast majority of my purchases, I automatically get 1% to 20% cash back. No extra effort—just the click of a button.

Rakuten also searches for any available coupons. It works well. For instance, between the coupons and the cash back, I often save more than $20 every time I buy running shoes. I also recently combined a Rakuten promotion with another promotion offered by one of my credit cards to buy 15 bottles of good wine for less than $30, including taxes and shipping. In other words, it cost only $2 per bottle for excellent wine! You can't even get Trader Joe's wine at that price anymore.

Free Money Tip #8: Minimize tax payments and file for a refund in February

Let's say you have $10,000 and you want to invest it. You start researching different options and narrow it down to the following three:

(1) Stock market index fund. Conservative expected return after fees: 7%
(2) Bond market index fund. Conservative expected return after fees: 4%
(3) The cigar box under your mattress. Conservative expected return after fees: 0%

This is not a trick question. Sure, an argument can be made that for some people (such as those who are in retirement or very risk-averse), the bond fund might make more sense than the stock fund. But no one is going to advocate for putting your money in a cigar box under your mattress. That's a terrible use of your money. You know that already.

But I suspect that you're doing the same thing every year with your taxes. If you get a refund every April, that's not something to celebrate. All it means is that you gave the government a loan that, like the cigar box under your mattress, earned you 0% interest.

You should try to update your tax forms every year to minimize the amount that is withheld from your paycheck. That maximizes the amount you have available for investing.

Similarly, if you do expect a refund, do not wait until April 15 to file your taxes. Don't ever file in January, as employers, banks, and others are usually not required to send you tax forms until January 31, and some forms are not due until the middle of February. If you file before then, you risk missing something and having to file a corrected tax return. But by the end of February, you should have all of the forms you need to file your tax return. If you expect a refund, file then, and put your money to work for you.

Free Money Tip #9:
Get a cash payment for refinancing private student loans

Many people carry significant student loan debt. That debt is usually a combination of federal and private loans. Those are two entirely different animals. Federal loans have a host of benefits that private loans do not.

One benefit of federal loans in particular — the Public Service Loan Forgiveness program — allows some borrowers, such as myself, to get literally hundreds of thousands of dollars in federal student loans wiped out entirely. No joke. You have to dot many I's and cross many T's, but these benefits are real.

And the Coronavirus Aid, Relief, and Economic Security (CARES) Act of 2020 included other significant benefits for federal student loan holders.

You could accidentally lose out on all of these and other benefits by refinancing federal loans. So make sure that you *do your research before refinancing federal student loans*. You can easily end up worse off, and even lose hundreds of thousands of dollars in potential benefits, by mishandling your federal student loans.

Private student loans, on the other hand, are generally much more straightforward and do not have the benefits that federal loans have. Like all loans, private student loans have either a fixed or a variable interest rate, and generally speaking that's all that matters when it comes to figuring out what private student loan is best for you.

This means that when national interest rates are low, as they are now, you may want to look into refinancing your private student loans. In 2021, some companies are offering rates for student loans that are as low as 4% or perhaps even lower.

The free money that comes from refinancing private student loans occurs because many companies are competing for your business. To try to win you over, they often offer cash payments upfront. These are usually anywhere from $200 to $500.

Now let me be clear: that small amount of money likely pales in comparison to what you're going to end up paying in interest over the life of the loan. So your primary goal in refinancing private student loans is to secure the lowest fixed interest rate possible.

If one company offers a 10-year loan at 4% interest with a $500 payment upfront, and another company offers the same loan at 3.75% but no cash payment, you will almost certainly be better off ignoring the $500 and instead taking the 3.75% interest rate! If you have any significant amount of student loans, you'll save way more money by having even a slightly better interest rate. But if the company offering the lowest interest rate also offers a cash bonus, then you can save on the loan and get free money at the same time.

Free Money Tip #10:
Check for unclaimed property

This sounds strange, I know, but you would be amazed at how many people have "unclaimed property" waiting for them at a state government's treasury office. And by "unclaimed property," I'm not talking about the socks that your dryer consumes every time you wash your clothes. I mean money. And it could be a significant amount of money.

For instance, if you have ever moved and changed jobs at the same time, it's possible that your last paycheck never made it to you. That doesn't mean your employer got to keep it. It means that this money may be waiting for you in the treasurer's office of the state you moved away from.

Go to the website of every state you've ever lived (and the state you live in now) and find out how to look up if you have unclaimed property.

Free Money Tip #11:
Ask your employer to reimburse you

You are not going to believe this, but I didn't get my first cell phone until 2018. That was at the age of 38 and a full 10 years into my career as a lawyer. I decided a long time ago that I didn't want to pay a monthly bill for a cell phone, and I learned how to get by without one. It wasn't easy, particularly when traveling, but I always figured it out.

And I probably still wouldn't have a cell phone now if it weren't for the fact that my work pays for it. In 2018, I went into a management position at a new agency, where they needed to be able to reach me when I was not in the office. So they bought the phone and they pay all of the monthly charges. This saves me hundreds of dollars in expenses that most people pay every year for a cell phone and plan.

If you work for someone else, think about every expense you incur that is work-related in any way. If there's an argument that the expense is work-related, you should ask your employer to pay for it. The worst they can do is say no. And you might be pleasantly surprised at what they say yes to.

For instance, when my state bar association asked me to give a presentation in another part of the state, I agreed to do it. I then realized that I was going to have to drive around 100 miles roundtrip to be at this speaking event, and it occurred to me that my employer might reimburse the mileage. I was curious, so I asked. They said yes. I've since done that same presentation every six months, in different parts of the state. Because I decided to ask that first time, I've been reimbursed hundreds of dollars that I would not have normally received.

Another thing to ask about is licensing and membership fees for professional organizations. These can add up to hundreds of dollars per year. If they are related in any way, or add any value, to the work you do, you should ask your employer to reimburse these expenses.

Think even more broadly. Do you ever check email and do other work from home? If so, maybe your employer would consider paying for your internet service.

What about your commute to work? Some employers pay for all or part of those expenses too.

You won't know until you ask.

Free Money Tip #12:
Get incentive payments from your health insurer

Despite what you've heard about health insurers, they sometimes have your best interests in mind. Not when a bill comes due. At that point, someone owes money to a hospital, and you and your insurer are poised for battle on who has to pay.

But before anyone goes to the hospital, your insurance company wants you to be healthy. That way you never end up in the hospital, and there's no bill for anyone to pay.

To incentivize you to get and stay healthy, many health insurance companies offer to pay you to do things that improve your health. This usually involves things like increasing the amount you exercise or improving your diet.

You may have been planning to do that anyway. Look into whether your insurance company will pay you to do it.

Free Money Tip #13:
Return purchases that do not meet expectations

Just about anything can be returned. And it should be if it's defective in any way. Whenever you buy something and it doesn't meet your expectations, return it. Electronics, clothes, vitamins, even groceries.

Yes, groceries. Don't make the mistake of thinking that just because you already used an item it can't be "returned." We once bought an expensive organic watermelon from our local co-op, only to cut into it and realize that it was rotten. We called the co-op and they gave us a refund. We obviously did not actually return the rotten watermelon. But we still got our money back.

Returning things is even more important for big-ticket items that fail to meet expectations. Ever buy a car and then realize it wasn't as great as you thought it would be? Check the laws in your state — you can probably return it, no questions asked, within the first few days.

Free Money Tip #14:
Ask your relatives to give cash rather than gifts

"Now this looks like a book," I said as I pulled a large rectangular gift from under the Christmas tree. The tag was in my dad's handwriting and read, "To Kyle. From Logan."

My dad's actual name is Neil, but he always likes to use gift tags to provide a clue about what's under the wrapping.

I turned to him and said, "Let me guess: the *Ultimate X-Men?*"

Everyone in the room started laughing.

My joke was a reference to the previous Christmas when my dad had given me a second copy of a book called *Ultimate X-Men.* He had somehow forgotten that he gave me that very same book the Christmas before.

It had become a revolving joke in my family that my dad gave me the same book for two years in a row. This was why my whole family chuckled when I joked about getting the *Ultimate X-Men* again.

As I went back to unwrapping the gift, I expected to see some new Wolverine collection that had just been released. Instead, I saw the word "Ultimate."

Hmmm, I thought, Dad must have found an *Ultimate Wolverine.* As I peeled away more wrapping, I saw the next word: "X-Men."

My siblings and I all started laughing harder than we had laughed in a long time. My dad had bought me the same book *three years in a row*.

Cash, Dad. Just give me cash. Every year. Every occasion. I will always know how to make better use of this money than you will.

If your relatives are great at giving gifts, that's wonderful. But if they usually mess it up, you should ask them to give cash, not gifts.

Free Money Tip #15: Return gifts

Guess what I did with those extra copies of *Ultimate X-Men*? I returned them, and each time I was amazed at the small fortune my dad had paid — three times over — for this book. It gave me a nice free shopping spree to get other books, movies, and music that I could actually use.

When it comes to weddings and baby showers, you hopefully set up a registry. (Or, when my partner and I got married, we decided we already had enough stuff and just gave people a list of charities for sending donations.)

But we all have a few friends or relatives that like to buy something that's not on the registry. This doesn't mean you're stuck with what they give you. Okay, if it's something homemade, then you're stuck with it. But if they bought you something, there should be a way to return it. Do it.

They're not going to find out. And even if they somehow did, they won't hate you because you returned their gift. (If they do, then they may not have been such a great friend in the first place.)

The benefit of returned gifts is exactly what this chapter promises for all of these tips: free money.

If you don't have a receipt, you're unlikely to get a cash refund. But you should at least get store credit. Unless the gift was from an airline catalog, you should be able to find something useful that you can buy with store credit. The best choice is always something that you would have had to spend money on anyway. The only exception is if the store sells Baby Yoda Chia Pets. Then that's your best choice because those things are adorable!

Free Money Tip #16: Get back deposits (with interest) and co-op payouts

Many businesses collect deposits when you open an account with them. Your property manager and utilities often require an upfront deposit.

This is a brilliant business strategy for the collector of the deposit. The collector gets to invest your money and make interest on it, often for many years. Additionally, in most instances, the deposit gets returned only when you move, and if you forget to ask for your deposit back, you may never get it.

Always insist on getting your deposit back. And make sure it's sent to the right place. If you just moved, you need to provide your property manager and utilities with your new address and follow up with them if they don't refund your deposit right away.

Yes, I know, getting deposits back is not really free money, since this is your own hard-earned cash in the first place. But it's still cash in hand that you can easily lose out on if you don't follow through and make sure you get it back.

If you start running into issues with getting a deposit back, look into your state's consumer protection laws. For instance, a number of states place short deadlines on property managers to return deposits, and those laws may even entitle you to a larger amount of money if the return of a deposit is delayed. Sometimes mentioning those laws to your property manager will get them to act a lot faster than they might otherwise do.

Turning to another type of free money — and this really is money that you never paid in the first place — if you belong to any co-ops, make sure you get any payouts they provide. Many grocery stores, electric utilities, and other businesses are co-ops.

If you are a member of a co-op, then you are an owner as well. This usually means that when the co-op makes more money than it anticipated (for instance, because it charges $17,000 for a bottle of barefoot-squeezed kombucha), that extra money goes back to members like you.

If you're a member of more than one co-op, you may be accumulating $100 or more every year in credits. For instance, our local food co-op refunds my family around $50 per year, and we also usually accumulate around $50 per year from our local electric utility.

The food co-op sends a check to us at the beginning of every year. A few times we've almost recycled the check without even opening the letter because we assumed it was junk mail!

Our electric utility keeps a running balance of how much we have accumulated. Although they return some of this money to current members at the end of every year (in the form of a bill credit), people can lose this money when they move.

Like your deposits, stay on top of these credits. Make sure you get paid your money.

Free Money Tip #17:
Make use of warranties if something breaks

Let me start by noting that I'm not advocating that you ever pay for an extended warranty. (See the end of my later chapter on insurance for why extended warranties are almost always a complete rip-off.) But you should pay attention to the warranty that automatically comes with whatever you're buying. For instance, many electronics automatically come with a one-year warranty.

Even better, did you know that a lot of credit cards *double* the warranty? As long as you bought the item on that card, a one-year warranty is now a two-year warranty. Remember this and call your credit card company if an item breaks within your card's extended warranty period.

This extended warranty is completely free. And it works — I once bought a digital camera on an American Express card. It had a one-year warranty and then broke just before the two-year mark. I immediately called American Express, and they refunded every dollar.

★ ★ ★

These 17 tips hopefully give you a few ideas of how to get some of the free money that is out there waiting for you every day. In the next few chapters, we'll talk about other ways to increase your income.

If you don't think you can remember all of these free money tips, don't worry — I've got you covered. They're all listed (with helpful hyperlinks) in my up-to-date checklist, which you can download for free at:

personalfinanceauthor.com

6

GET A RAISE NOW

Whatever your job currently pays you, it is not enough. You are worth *far* more than that.

How do I know this? Two reasons. First, you're reading this book. That means you're smart. Smart people deserve to be paid more because they bring more value to their work. Second, we're all underpaid. Everyone deserves a raise.

Unless your employer is required to keep you employed, you presumably are still in your job because you bring value to the workplace. You need to make sure you're getting fairly compensated for the value you bring. Getting a raise is the single biggest thing you can do to improve your financial circumstances. Let's talk about how to do it.

To get a raise, you need to learn the mechanics of how to negotiate. The best way to do this is to read Ramit Sethi's book *I Will Teach You to be Rich*. Make sure you get the most up-to-date version. Flip to the chapter on getting a raise. (Then go back and read the whole book — it's excellent.) Ramit Sethi's book contains actual scripts on how to negotiate a better salary. The scripts are based on a significant body of research, and they work.

The basic idea is simple. It's three steps. First, you need to be a top performer. In other words, you need to deserve a raise. Second, you need to convince yourself you deserve a raise. This lets you show your boss that you're a top performer. Third, you need to ask for a raise now.

Step 1: Deserve a raise

If you're terrible at your job, you're not going to get a raise. And yes, this applies even to union workers, government workers, and every other group that you might think gets raises for doing nothing. Even if your workplace provides cost-of-living adjustments or step increases to everyone, the larger pay raises are only available to high performers.

You need to be a top performer. It would take a separate book to describe what makes someone a high performer in the workplace. And my guess is that you already know what it takes.

I'll just throw out a few basic concepts that, in my experience, always increase your value as an employee:

- Be enjoyable to work with. Your boss will ask your co-workers about you. If you're nice to your co-workers and they enjoy working with you, your employer will want to keep you. By contributing to a healthy workplace environment, you bring great value.

- Be a good listener. You need to listen to your co-workers to know how to make things better at your workplace. And I mean all of your co-workers, regardless of status. Yes, know what your boss wants. But also know what the janitor thinks can be improved.

- Work hard. You need to be willing to put in longer hours than others. Not every day. Not even every week. But at least once a month, you should burn the midnight oil. This shows dedication. And your boss will likely pay you more for working longer hours.

- Do great work. Although you don't want to become a perfectionist, always lean toward quality over quantity. You want your co-workers and super-visors to know that your work product is top-notch. Review and copy-edit everything (even emails) at least once.

- Continually improve. You need a growth mindset to stand out in the work-place. If a supervisor tears apart something you wrote, don't get upset. Be grateful for the learning opportunity. Read the edits carefully to find out how you can do better next time.

- Make everyone around you shine. Never miss an opportunity to show grat-itude for something a co-worker does. Give others credit every time. Down-play your contributions and play up theirs.

- Admit to mistakes when they happen. Nobody is perfect. You will make mistakes at the workplace — guaranteed. Own up to these mistakes. Take full responsibility for them. You'd be amazed at how much trust this builds among your co-workers.

- Volunteer to do the things no one else wants to do. Not every time — you don't want to make yourself miserable just to improve your standing at work. But make yourself known as someone who is willing to take on the less desirable work so that others don't have to.

- Follow through on every work assignment. Try to meet deadlines, but if you can't, just let your supervisor know. Apologize for the delay and keep them in the loop. Communication goes a long way. Don't ignore an assignment and hope your boss forgets about it. Be reliable. Be responsible.

- Stand up for others. If you ever see anyone being treated poorly, stand up for them. Every time. It doesn't matter how much higher up the person is who is doing the mistreating. Tell them that their behavior is not okay. Be an upstander, not a bystander.

Step 2: Convince yourself you deserve a raise

Whether you're into affirmations or not, remind yourself every day that *you are worth more to your employer than they are worth to you.*

That's a fact. They chose to hire you. They have also chosen to not fire you. They're keeping you employed because you bring them value — more value than if you did not work for them.

My partner is the one who helped me realize that I am not lucky to have a job. Rather, my employer is lucky to have me.

My partner has held a number of self-employed and contract positions over the years. I still remember overhearing her on the phone with one of her employers and being amazed at how confidently she bargained for the terms she needed to make it worth continuing to work for this employer.

Her self-advocacy surprised me because I had always thought that only the employer makes demands. It was my view that the employee's job was to follow those demands (or seek work elsewhere if the demands were unreasonable).

Here was my partner calmly explaining that she worked hard, did good work, and needed better pay if she was going to continue doing that good work. Nothing she said should have surprised me. It was all true. I had just never thought of it that way.

When I heard her explain this to her employer, it clicked: her employer was lucky to have her. The employer knew it too, and they gave her everything she asked for.

When I saw my partner advocate for herself this way, I knew that I should do the same myself. For some reason, I had thought it was too uppity to advocate for oneself in the workplace. I thought this would put my job at risk. After all, my employer, by definition, can fire me at any time. But my partner helped me see that I also can fire my employer at any time.

Humility aside, I have always been an outstanding employee. My work is top-notch, and people enjoy working with me. Every one of my employers has received way more value out of me than whatever they've paid me. I remind myself of this every time I ask for a raise.

If you do the same, you'll greatly increase your chances of getting a raise. Advocating for yourself does not put you at risk of being fired. Far from it. When you advocate for yourself, it tells your employer that you know you're worth more than what they're paying you. This makes you all the more valuable to your employer. That makes you all the more likely to get a raise.

Finally, if you have any doubt about whether you deserve a raise, you can always apply for another job and find out what a new employer would pay you. Obviously, you need to think long and hard before doing this, and I would never recommend applying for another job just to give yourself more leverage with your current employer. This can burn bridges with the company you apply to, and you might end up also losing credibility with your current employer if they see that you don't ever plan to leave your current job. Only apply for a new job if you plan to take it.

If you do change jobs, you might get a big raise. Switching jobs often leads to much larger salary increases than staying with your current employer. Also, when you get another job offer, if you decide you might prefer to stay with your current employer, it completely changes the dynamics of negotiating your salary. It is very common for employers to match (or improve upon) a competitor's offer to avoid losing one of their best employees. You deserve the best deal, so let your current employer and the potential one compete for you and see who offers the most.

Step 3: Ask now

Not tomorrow. Today.

Yes, you need to do some planning on how you're going to get a raise. But don't overthink it.

Asking for a raise can be scary. It can be uncomfortable. Because of that, you'll think about every reason *not* to do it. Maybe you'll convince yourself that because you're so great at your job, there's no need to ask for a raise — your boss will come to you and offer you more money.

If you find yourself coming up with excuses for inaction, you need to stop that train of thought. Remind yourself that you deserve a raise. You did Steps 1 and 2 already. It's time to put your plan into action.

When you ask for a raise, it's helpful if you come prepared with a specific number and a justification for it. For instance, if you know what colleagues make, that is a useful data point. There are also lots of helpful online resources to determine the average salary for people in your field of work. Three of the most common websites are PayScale, Salary, and Glassdoor.

One more note on asking for raises. Research shows that, unfortunately, there's a significant gender gap regarding which employees ask for raises. In short, men are much more likely to ask for raises than women. Not because they are any more deserving. Far from it.

Researchers have discovered a similar phenomenon in applying for jobs: men are much more likely to apply for jobs even when they do not meet the minimum qualifications for the job, while women take those minimum qualifications more seriously.

I mention this research for two reasons.

First, if you're a woman, it's all the more important that you ask for raises on a regular basis. You deserve it — as much, if not more than your male colleagues who are asking for raises every chance they get.

Unfortunately, you may have had a bad experience asking for raises in the past. This should never happen, but I know several women who have been through this. Your boss may have treated you differently than male colleagues who asked for similar raises. If that has happened, then you may understandably want to proceed with caution, particularly if you're still with the same employer. For instance, you may want to have a trusted colleague talk to your boss first about why you deserve a raise. Also, if you suspect any form of discrimination whatsoever, you should document everything you can, in case you end up in a legal dispute at a later time.

This brings me to my second point about the gender gap when it comes to asking for and receiving raises. If you're one of the fortunate few who is in management, then take it upon yourself to right this wrong. Make sure you set up a system of regular annual reviews for all employees. This is the best way to ensure that every employee has an equal opportunity at a raise, regardless of whether they ask for it.

This chapter hopefully makes you feel empowered to ask for a raise. Do it now. You won't regret it, and it may just change your life. An increased salary will do more to improve your finances than just about anything else.

7

FIND YOUR SIDE HUSTLE

Your day job will likely be your main source of income for most of your life. That's why you want to use the techniques from the previous chapter to make sure you're maximizing the amount of income you get from your day job. This chapter is about how to supplement that income with a side hustle.

But first, let's talk about how *not* to do a side hustle. This dad story dates back to when I was in elementary school and I woke up every morning to a high-pitched voice squeaking the following words over and over (and over):

"Hi! Good morning! Wake up! Wake up!"

The source of this racket was a Mickey Mouse alarm clock that my dad had won during a "poker night" for a charity fundraiser. He gave the alarm clock to my sister. The thing was so loud that I would hear it from my room across the hallway.

It completely ruined Mickey Mouse for me. I think it ruined alarm clocks for me as well. Come to think of it, maybe this is why I've trained myself to wake up early every morning so that I never have to set an alarm clock.

The Mickey Mouse alarm clock was not the only thing my dad won at this fundraiser. He also won a giant teddy bear and some other random (and equally worthless) things.

To be clear, everything he won had been donated to the fundraiser. And someone was going to win each item, so it's not like my dad cost the charity money. In fact, the charity profited from the money my dad paid to purchase poker chips at the beginning of the night.

The way my dad cleaned house at this fundraiser was by playing blackjack. The blackjack dealer was a volunteer. He was dealing out only one deck of cards, and he only reshuffled the cards after all of them had been played. Anyone who knows blackjack knows that it's fairly easy to turn the odds in your favor when there's only one deck of cards. All you do is watch how many aces and high cards come out in the early rounds, and bet low when lots of the good cards have been played. Then you bet high when only low cards have been played (since that's when lots of good cards remain). Casinos have figured out how to prevent players from doing this. Casinos often use at least six decks of cards, and they also prohibit counting cards. But the poker night fundraiser was not quite as sophisticated.

My dad's success at the blackjack table is the closest he's come to a side hustle. And I don't think anyone else in my family considered it a success in any way. As I mentioned earlier, the alarm clock did not improve mornings at our home. It still gives me nightmares. I have no idea what happened to the giant teddy bear or any of the other things my dad won. On top of this, my mom was, of course, completely mortified that my dad had taken advantage of a local fundraiser.

Fortunately, there are much better side hustles out there! Let's talk about some of the side hustles that, unlike my dad's ventures, will bring in real money and will do so on a regular basis.

Side hustles come in many forms but generally fall into two categories: (1) passive income, and (2) active income.

We all know what active income is. That's your day job, where you exchange your time for money. If you stop working, you stop getting paid.

Passive income is entirely different. This is putting your money to work for you. The idea is that you do work upfront and then relax and collect payments while you sleep.

Let's start with side hustles that create passive income, as those are by far the best side hustles you can get.

Passive side hustles

Let me tell you a quick story involving a particular type of passive income — royalties — that I missed out on when I was young. Royalties, whether from photo rights, patents, books, music, designs, or anything else, are passive income because they require work upfront, and then provide income while you sleep.

When I was in high school, a family friend called to tell my parents that he had seen a photo of me on the back of a cereal box. I couldn't believe it. I was going to be rich!

Let me back up a minute. You're probably wondering how on earth my photo ended up on the back of a cereal box.

At the age of 15, an ad agency selected me to be in a Kellogg's Frosted Flakes commercial. Yes, with Tony the Tiger. They were looking for young athletes, and I was an aspiring whitewater kayaker and somehow ended up getting chosen for this commercial. I still remember one of my high-school classmates being genuinely perplexed by this. She bluntly asked me, "Why'd they choose you? Why not, I don't know, someone *hotter*?"

I didn't know the answer then, and I still don't know it now. But they did choose me, and it turned out to be a fascinating experience.

The ad agency flew me out to California (first class!) and paid me an hourly wage for three days of filming. I think it was $75 per hour, which, come to think of it, is more than I've ever made doing anything else!

I also got royalties every time the commercial aired. This provided a steady stream of passive income. Not bad for a high-school kid, although it was only enough to cover my kayaking expenses at the time.

"The real money is if you end up on a cereal box," the producer had told me. He said this while we were taking a break during the filming of the commercial. I was talking to him under a shade tent that had been set up just for him. The crew had found a relatively flat area on the side of the river where they could place his tent and oversized chair. Despite everything that had been done to accommodate him, he still complained about having to be outdoors for the filming. I remember him telling me that his idea of "roughing it" was "going to bed at night and not finding a mint on my pillow." When he talked about how cereal boxes provide the biggest royalties, he told me that this was "the kind of thing that will pay for college."

So when I heard that I had made it onto a cereal box, I knew I was going to be rich!

Then the same photos of me also started showing up in magazines and comic books! This was amazing. I went to a local pharmacy and searched every comic book they had. My picture was in over 20 of them! As I handed $40 to the person at the cash register, I thought that I wasn't really paying $40, because I was going to get royalties back from every sale. An automatic discount!

As the weeks passed, I kept waiting for the first royalty check to arrive. And waiting.

After a few months, I started wondering what was going on. Had they lost my address?

I found a phone number for someone at the ad agency and called them to find out when I would get my royalty checks for the cereal boxes, magazines, and comic books. When they finally got back to me, they told me that there would be no checks.

"What?" I said. "The producer told me that if I got on a cereal box, it would pay for college."

They then explained to me that while the commercial was being filmed, they had contacted my parents about photo rights. My parents had signed away *all* photo rights for *all* time in exchange for $1,500.

Now, to be fair, this one was not my parents' fault. The ad agency took advantage of them. Also, I remember my parents asking me about this at the time it happened. I didn't ever see the contract, but I recall my parents saying, "They want us to sign something so they can take photos of you, and then they'll pay us another $1,500." It sounded great, so I agreed.

But the end result was that I never received a penny in royalties for the photos that were used on cereal boxes, comic books, magazines, and anywhere else the ad agency put them. If my parents had negotiated even a tiny percentage of royalties for the use of these photos, I might be rich now.

Lesson learned. Royalties matter. Never give up a form of ongoing passive income for a one-time payment.

Royalties are just one form of passive income. There are many other forms of passive income that will make you money while you sleep. For instance, real estate investments can provide passive income if you find a deal that provides enough money to hire a property manager. I've got a separate chapter on real estate later in this book.

Your portfolio investments are also a form of passive income. When your investments increase, you can receive dividends or sell stocks and bonds at a profit from what you paid to buy them.

But you'll want to think more broadly than that. When you think about how to make money with a side hustle, start by brainstorming anything and everything you can do to bring in passive income. If you need more ideas about ways to bring in passive income, there are lots of great books on this topic. One of my favorites is *Passive Income, Aggressive Retirement*, by Rachel Richards. (Her first book, *Money Honey*, is another great read.)

The greatest thing about passive income side hustles is you can usually do them at your own pace. If you're seeking royalties by writing a book or working on a patent, you can squeeze that in whenever you have free time.

The downside, of course, is that you never know if your passive income side hustle will bring in enough money to be worth it. For instance, you could write the great American novel, but if no one recognizes it as such until after you've left this world (which seems to be the pattern for most great American novels), you might never make any money.

For this reason, I recommend looking for passive income side hustles that you truly enjoy. If you love writing, do it. If you love real estate, do it. Let the activity be a reward in itself, and then any money that flows from it is just a bonus.

Active side hustles

A more consistent way to bring in extra money is through active side hustles. Some of the most popular active side hustles are driving for Uber or Lyft, making home deliveries, and walking or boarding dogs with an app like Rover. There are also active side hustles that can be done remotely, such as copy-editing and freelance writing. These, of course, take work.

Like your day job, active side hustles require you to trade your time for money. Generally speaking, the more time you trade, the more you'll make. And as soon as you stop working, you stop bringing in extra income.

Let me begin by saying that I'm not a big fan of active side hustles. But this is for personal reasons. My day job already has me working long hours, and I prefer to spend my free time with my family. Also, I have a good track record of getting raises consistently at work, and those raises often provide more income than an active side hustle would. So for me, I'd rather focus my work time on my day job and getting paid more for that work.

Also, I live in a rural part of Vermont. (Is that redundant?) Most active side hustles, like Uber and Lyft, work only in big cities. The options are much more limited for those of us who live in rural areas. Still, even if you live in a rural area, there are lots of active side hustles that can be done remotely, like copy-editing and freelance writing.

If you have time and energy and want to jumpstart your journey to financial freedom, active side hustles may be just the thing. There are many stories out there about people who took on multiple side hustles and made enormous leaps in their journey toward financial independence.

The reason active side hustles can improve your finances so much is that the reward is often doubled. First, you make extra income and therefore have more to invest. Second, because you're so busy working two, three, four, or even more jobs, you spend way less. You simply don't have time to do the activities you used to spend money on. You can't go clubbing when you're delivering groceries to someone else's house.

If you're interested in active side hustles, do some research to find out all the options that are out there. Although you want to find ones that pay the best, you should also keep in mind that it's not always easy to tell what you'll make until you start doing it.

This is because the pay for many of these activities is not hourly. Rather, it depends on how much work you get and how quickly and efficiently you can perform tasks. For instance, a lot of freelance editing websites advertise a decent rate like $20 per hour, but then a quick Google search reveals that most people actually make far less than that.

For these reasons, I recommend assuming that your hourly rate will be fairly low. Accept that and look for other things that will make this work worthwhile. Here are two things to consider:

(1) **What do you like doing?** If you love driving, think about Lyft and Uber. Yes, it's still going to be work. That's why you're getting paid for it. But if it's something that's enjoyable, you're a lot more likely to stick with it.

(2) **What are you already doing?** Maybe you already walk your dog for an hour every day. If there's a Rover customer nearby, you might be able to grab their dog and get paid for something you were going to be doing anyway! Same for food deliveries. The savviest side hustlers sign up for multiple food deliveries and then time their commute home to coincide with making a delivery or two.

Just about every story of financial independence involves side hustles. And there are new ones out there every day. Find the ones that work for you and get started.

8

GET REAL (ESTATE)

O ne of the most reliable paths to making more money is real estate. Some say that real estate has created far more millionaires than everything else combined.

Everyone should look into real estate, at least for their own home, and they should also look into investing in additional properties. It's not for everyone, and it does carry significant risk. But if you're serious about financial independence, you're going to want to look into — and learn about — investing in real estate.

Buying your home

Remember at the beginning of this book when I mentioned how my family bought a house with 103% financing? Most financial advisors will tell you that this was a bad move. You have to save at least 20% for a down payment before you buy a house, right?

Wrong. You don't need a 20% down payment. Many banks provide mortgages when the buyer has far less money (or even no money) down.

A 20% down payment has two main benefits: (1) you avoid having to pay mortgage insurance, and (2) you have immediate equity in your house. Those are both significant benefits, but let's dig a little deeper.

With my family's house, it's true that we had to pay mortgage insurance, but we locked in such a low mortgage rate (3.5%) that even with mortgage insurance, our effective rate was still an incredibly low 4%. If we had waited to build up a 20% down payment, we could have ended up with a much higher interest rate.

I've heard stories of the days when people paid an interest rate of over 12% for a mortgage! Run any mortgage calculator and you will be amazed at the difference even ¼ of a percentage point makes, let alone entire percentage points. The benefits of locking in a low interest rate when you buy cannot be overstated.

As for equity, I knew that on the day we bought our house, it was worth at least 20% more than what we paid for it. We had been casually looking at real estate for a few years, and the moment we saw a $200,000 house on the market for $160,000, we jumped on it. We started out with the same equity as most other homeowners, but without having to spend $40,000.

In the seven years that we've owned our house, our home value has gone up another $40,000.

This is not surprising. In fact, assuming that the home was worth $200,000 when we bought it, a value of $240,000 just seven years later reflects an appreciation rate of around 3%. That's on the lower end of how much home values typically appreciate.

So we now have a $240,000 home. And we only owe $140,000 on it. This is because, even though we borrowed over $160,000 to buy the house, we had such a low interest rate on our mortgage that we've been able to pay off more than $20,000 in principal.

So after just seven years of homeownership, we built up around $100,000 of equity. This consisted of $40,000 at the time of purchase (by finding a home priced less than it was worth), $40,000 in appreciation, and $20,000 in payments toward principal.

We got this $100,000 in equity for a monthly payment that (including property taxes, insurance, and repairs) was not much more than what we had been paying in rent. Had we continued renting during these seven years, we would have saved some money in monthly payments, but investing those savings would not have given us anywhere near what we were able to build up in equity by buying a home.

All told, we now have $100,000 in financial net worth that we would not have if we had been renting.

I tell this story because it illustrates a key lesson about all real estate: *buy houses that are worth more than they cost*. You make money in the purchase of real estate, not in the selling. Get equity right off the bat and you're far more likely to end up doing well on your investment.

Now let me be clear: homeownership is not for everyone. Do your research before you buy a home. For many people, such as those planning to move in the next five years, renting may be a better option. When you buy a home and resell it within five years, you usually lose more money on transaction costs than you make. So if you're going to move in the next five years, you're almost always better off renting.

If you decide you do want to buy a home, take your time looking for one. This is an incredibly complex and emotional process. It involves many factors, including what school district you'll be in if you have kids. Don't rush into the first thing you find. The longer you have to look around at what's for sale, the smarter you'll be at finding a good deal.

When you're ready to make an offer, make sure your contract includes an inspection provision. I would never buy real estate "as is." Hire the best home inspector in your area, no matter the cost. They'll find things that you need to know about, and you'll probably get your money back (and then some) in post-inspection negotiations. Remember that if the house has a well and a septic system, the inspector should be checking those too.

And also make sure your lawyer knows how to do a title search. If the property was ever a gas station, laundromat, or any other business that dealt in any way with hazardous chemicals of any kind, do not buy the property. Ever.

There is no faster way to lose money than to buy a contaminated property. Trust me — I used to bring these types of lawsuits on behalf of a state environmental agency to get properties cleaned up. If you think replacing a boiler is expensive, try remediating contamination that a previous owner created. Stay far, far away from properties that are potentially contaminated.

Should I get a 30-year mortgage or a 15-year mortgage?

When you buy a home, a 30-year mortgage may be the only option if you cannot afford a higher monthly payment. But if you do have a choice, you need to decide whether to get a 30-year mortgage or a 15-year mortgage. Actually, you usually have even more options than that. Perhaps the most overlooked option is a 20-year mortgage. My partner and I discovered the 20-year mortgage when we recently refinanced our house.

Each option comes with trade-offs. This is one of those areas where I think of what Mindy Jensen of the *BiggerPockets Money Podcast* always says: "personal finance really is personal."

For some people, a 30-year mortgage makes the most sense. For others, it's a 15-year mortgage. Or, as my partner and I recently discovered, what made the most sense for us was a 20-year mortgage.

Most financial advisors recommend 30-year mortgages. The theory is that mortgages are "the cheapest money out there." This has never been truer than in 2021 when those with good credit can get 30-year mortgages with rates as low as 3% or less. If you can secure a mortgage rate that low, then this is usually your best bet.

The biggest benefit to a 30-year mortgage is that it minimizes your monthly payment. That frees up more money for other priorities, like investing in your retirement accounts.

If, for instance, your investments make an average rate of return of 7% (which they hopefully will), then you're better off getting a 30-year mortgage and putting more money toward investments.

Note that, by this theory, you should pay only your monthly mortgage payment. Some people try to pay down their mortgages faster by paying extra each month, or by setting up half-payments every two weeks (which means 13 monthly payments per year, rather than 12). I'm not a big fan of this strategy.

If you want to pay off your mortgage in less than 30 years, then you should look into getting a 15-year or 20-year mortgage right off the bat to get the lowest interest rate possible. If you instead decide on a 30-year mortgage and you have a low interest rate like 3%, 4%, or even 5%, then you might as well just stick with that and send any extra money you have into investments.

That said, you shouldn't get a 30-year mortgage just because that's what most people do. Nor should you do it just because most financial advisors tell you that a 30-year mortgage is the way to go. Financial advisors often have a natural bias toward 30-year mortgages because they know that this gives their clients much more money to invest every month, and your investments are where financial advisors usually make their money.

Also, most of the advice that touts the benefits of 30-year mortgages is outdated. In particular, the proponents of 30-year mortgages talk about the benefits of getting a tax deduction for the interest you pay on your mortgage. In my opinion, this was a dubious "benefit" to begin with. Yes, it's nice to get back a portion of the interest you pay. But of course, it's better to not pay that interest in the first place!

At any rate, this has become a moot point for most homeowners. This is because the Tax Cut and Jobs Act of 2017 significantly increased the standard deduction, making that the preferred option for around 90% of tax filers. If you're taking the standard deduction, you are not itemizing your deductions, and you get no benefit whatsoever from the interest you pay on your mortgage.

Consider a 20-year or a 15-year mortgage

Although most people have never even heard of 20-year mortgages, they deserve a serious look, as do 15-year mortgages. Remember that there's no single right answer here. For your situation, going with a 30-year mortgage may make the most sense, but you'll want to explore each option.

When my partner and I were refinancing our home last year, we found that a 20-year mortgage ticked all the boxes. I'll mention three reasons why we chose a 20-year mortgage rather than a 30-year mortgage.

First, you get a better rate than a 30-year mortgage. A difference of just ¼ of a point (for instance, 2.75% rather than 3%) can save you thousands, or even tens of thousands, of dollars in interest.

Second, you also save tens of thousands of dollars in interest by paying off your mortgage 10 years earlier. During years 21 through 30, you're not paying any interest at all because you're done!

Whenever you're looking at mortgages, you'll want to look at an online mortgage calculator and run some comparisons.

So, for instance, let's say you're buying or refinancing a $250,000 home and you pay $50,000 down. You need a mortgage to cover the remaining $200,000.

If you take out a 30-year mortgage at 3%, you'll end up paying $103,555 in interest. But if you can swing a 20-year mortgage at 2.75%, then you'll end up paying only $60,240 in interest. That's $43,315 you save in interest payments! Not to mention you're done 10 years earlier.

Third, you build up equity faster with a 20-year mortgage. People often pay off mortgages early because they're selling or refinancing their home. If you end up selling or refinancing your home before you've paid off your mortgage, you'll have much more equity if you're on a 20-year mortgage than a 30-year mortgage.

This is perhaps the most overlooked, but crucial, factor in choosing a mortgage. We often assume we'll pay off the entire mortgage according to its terms, but far more often we pay it off early, either because we're moving or refinancing. At the time of sale or refinancing, the more equity you have, the more money that goes into your pocket.

Consider the above example of a 30-year mortgage on $200,000 at 3% versus a 20-year mortgage at 2.75%. Let's say that this homeowner sells their property (or refinances) after 15 years. If they were on a 30-year mortgage, then they would still owe $120,483. But if they were on a 20-year mortgage, they would only owe $57,878. By choosing a 20-year mortgage, this person would have built up an extra $62,605 in equity!

If a 20-year mortgage sounds good, you're probably wondering why you wouldn't just go ahead and get a 15-year mortgage.

It's true that all of the benefits of a 20-year mortgage are even greater if you go with a 15-year mortgage. That said, a 15-year mortgage comes with a very high monthly payment. If you can afford to make that payment every month, then a 15-year mortgage may be the right choice.

Let's dive into the numbers a little more. Sticking with the same example of a $200,000 mortgage, the monthly payment on a 30-year term at 3% is $843. (Note that this is only for principal and interest. Your actual monthly payment could be much higher if you make escrow payments toward insurance and property taxes.) On a 20-year mortgage at 2.75%, the monthly payment rises to $1,084. But if you go with a 15-year mortgage at 2.5%, it goes up to $1,334.

So when you go from a 30-year mortgage to a 20-year mortgage, you have to pay an extra $241 per month, but you shave off 10 years of payments, $43,315 in interest, and build up equity much faster. But to go from a 20-year mortgage to a 15-year mortgage, you have to pay another $250 per month, and you shave off only five years of payments and $20,196 in interest. In other words, you pay more to get half the amount of benefits.

Also, let's look at what would happen if you go with the 20-year mortgage at $1,084 per month and then invest the extra $250 per month you're saving by not doing a 15-year mortgage. Even if you made only 4% on your investments, you'd build up $60,071 in your portfolio after 15 years. Since you'd only owe $57,878 on your 20-year mortgage, you could pay off your house in full at that point! And if your investments make more than 4% (and they probably would), you'd make a profit compared to signing up for a 15-year mortgage.

So I think a 20-year mortgage is always worth considering. But you'll need to do what's right for you. Here's a summary of all the numbers we just talked about with borrowing $200,000 through a 30-year, 20-year, or 15-year mortgage:

	30-YEAR	20-YEAR	15-YEAR
Interest Rate	3.00%	2.75%	2.5%
Total Interest Paid	$103,555	$60,240	$40,044
Years Saved from 30	0	10	15
Owed at 15 Years	$120,483	$57,878	$0
Monthly Payment	$843	$1,084	$1,334

Let me say one more thing about amortization and equity. Before we bought our first home, I naively thought that a 3% mortgage meant that when you got your monthly bill, if you owed $1,000 that month, you would have to pay another 3% in interest. So I thought that you would owe $1,030, with $1,000 going toward principal and $30 going to the bank as interest.

Needless to say, that is definitely not how mortgages work! The 3% is assessed against the total amount owed. So when you take out a $200,000 mortgage, you're going to pay around $6,000 in interest in the first year alone. That's $500 per month. Just to cover the interest.

The division of your payments (between interest and principal) doesn't matter if you end up holding the loan for its entire term. But this rarely happens. Most of us end up selling or at least refinancing our homes before we pay off our initial mortgage.

You always want to look at amortization schedules to see how quickly (or, more accurately, how slowly) you'll build up equity in your home. Look five, 10, 15, and 20 years out and see how much equity you'll actually have at that point. It's usually far less than you'd think. And this is while interest rates are at historic lows. If they go back up to 5%, 6%, 7%, or even higher, then traditional 30-year mortgages will have you paying mostly interest for many years.

It's important to build up home equity if you can. More equity means more options. For instance, if you ever need to do a major home repair, or pay for unforeseen medical expenses, you may want to use a home equity loan. Your ability to do so depends, of course, on how much equity you have.

Home equity can also be a form of insurance. Some people use home equity as a substitute for purchasing costly long-term care insurance. The idea is that if you own a $400,000 home outright before you retire, then you may not need to purchase long-term care insurance. Instead, if you ever need to go into a nursing home, you (or more likely your family) could sell your home and use the proceeds to pay for your nursing home expenses.

Home equity always gives you more options.

Investing in real estate

Real estate can also be a great way to increase your income. Rental real estate is an excellent source of passive income, particularly if you can find properties that pay enough rent to allow you to hire a property manager. Then it becomes truly passive income.

There are thousands of people who have leveraged a small amount of money into a real estate portfolio that brings in a passive income stream of rental money. These rentals bring in cash flow when they bring in more money than they cost after all expenses are taken into account.

For people who own enough rental properties, that cash flow can pay more than what most of us make at our day job. And many of these real estate investors hire property managers. This means that they may only need to spend an hour or so each month on their properties. Compare that to the usual 9–5 grind!

If you enjoy looking at and taking care of properties, you should definitely look into real estate investments. I won't try to cover that topic in this book — there are far more comprehensive guides out there if this investment option interests you. One place to start would be BiggerPockets, which has an in-depth website, blog forums, and hundreds of free podcasts on investing in real estate.

9

YOU CAN ALWAYS LEARN MORE

When I was around 10 years old, we traveled to the San Francisco Bay area to visit an uncle and his family. My uncle met us at the airport. However, since there were five of us (not including my uncle), we knew we couldn't fit in my uncle's car, so we had arranged a rental. My uncle waited for us to get in our rental car, and then we followed him as we drove out of the airport.

About half an hour later, my uncle's car pulled into a driveway. My mom pulled in right behind him and said something about how the house didn't look right. Then someone — who was *not* my uncle — got out of the car we had been following.

Oops.

Although none of us could pinpoint exactly when my mom had lost my uncle's car and started following a complete stranger, we figured that it had to have happened on the highway. We still give my mom lots of grief for this one whenever we visit my uncle.

My siblings and I are all big fans of Douglas Adams, so we likened my mom's navigating to Dirk Gently's "Zen" navigation method: find someone who looks like they know where they're going and follow them.

I tell this story about my mom mainly because this book already has so many stories about my dad, and I wouldn't want my mom to feel left out. Not really. My mom embarrasses easily, so I suspect she would have been just fine with me leaving her out of this book altogether.

The real reason I tell this story is because it illustrates the importance of following the right people. That's a crucial lesson for anyone who seeks to improve their financial situation.

It's also a lesson that, sadly, far too many people learn the hard way. Dive into the world of personal finance, and you will find story after story of people being swindled into horrible investments because they followed someone else's bad advice. Don't let this be you.

Your finances will greatly improve the smarter you get about how personal finance works and about how to optimize your money.

For instance, the chapters on investing in Part IV of this book explain an incredibly simple system that is aimed at maximizing your returns while minimizing the amount of time and energy required of you. But that is just a few chapters in one book. And you will probably find some of the information in that chapter counterintuitive, which will make you skeptical. You'll probably think, "Why on earth should I invest in boring low-fee index funds when Warren Buffett knows how to make much more money?"

This is good — I want you to be skeptical. That's one of the best financial habits you can have!

But skepticism does not mean rejecting anything you're unsure of. It means you need to do more research to see if it makes sense. In my upcoming chapters on investing, I mention a few books (like J.L. Collins' *The Simple Path to Wealth*) that explain in detail why so many smart people (including Warren Buffett himself) recommend investing in low-fee index funds. Don't take my word for it — go read those books yourself!

At the back of this book, I've listed many additional resources. Books, podcasts, websites, blogs. Whatever media works best for you, I recommend continuing to educate yourself about personal finance.

And you don't need to spend much money at all to do this. An enormous amount of material, including every podcast, website, and blog that I recommend, is available for free. As are any books and audiobooks that you can get from your local library. (Remember that if they don't have it, they should be able to get it for you through an interlibrary loan.)

What's great about this type of education is that it not only costs very little, but it usually ends up making you far more money than you spend. For instance, whatever amount of money you paid for this book (if you paid anything at all, rather than borrowing it), you've probably made that money back by now. And hopefully far more!

10

GIVE YOURSELF CREDIT

So I know I've told a lot of stories about how bad my dad is with money. Well, there's one area where he's actually quite good. That's credit scores. For as long as I can remember, my dad has known what it takes to get a good credit score, and he has made sure he did those things.

Of course, a cynic might point out that my dad's success in achieving good credit has hurt his finances more than it has helped him. Credit card companies and banks are eager to loan my dad money, and he's eager to take it. As a result, he has spent most of his life in debt!

So if you want to have a good credit score so you can spend more, let me stop you right there. A good credit score is not an excuse to spend money on things you don't need. Rather, a good credit score is what *saves* you money when spending on things you do need.

Good credit helps with everything. Want to buy a house or a car? If you have good credit, you'll pay lots in interest, but if you have bad credit, you'll pay a whole lot more. Perhaps even tens of thousands of dollars more over the life of the loan.

And good credit even affects things like the premiums you pay for car and life insurance. Or whether a property manager decides to let you rent from them. Believe it or not, employers might even look at your credit report before deciding whether to hire you.

Do not mess up your credit. And if it's already too late, you need to prioritize fixing any past mistakes and rebuilding your way to a better credit score.

Start by getting your credit reports and your credit score. You need to know where you are. Luckily, this is both easy and free. To get your credit reports from all three major credit institutions, go to annualcreditreport.com.

Use that exact website and no other. You can get all three reports once a year for free, and this does not have any negative impact on your credit score. I recommend getting all three at once the first time you do this, so you can see what the different reports look like and find out if you have any bad marks on any of your reports. If you do, see what you can do to fix them immediately.

Note that your credit reports won't include your credit score. To get that, I recommend using either Mint or Credit Karma. Both of these websites are free, and both provide you free access to your credit score. These websites are also great resources on exactly what goes into a credit score and what you can do to improve your score.

Here's a handy chart of the factors that go into your credit score and some specific tips for improving that part of your score:

Factor	Tips
Payment history (35%) Paying bills on time.	Pay every bill on time every time. I highly recommend setting up autopayments.
Credit utilization (30%) How much of your credit you use relative to the maximum amount you could use.	Increase your credit limit, but keep your expenditures low. You read that right. You want higher credit limits. Just don't spend it.
Credit history length (15%) How long you have held different accounts.	That credit card you got in college to get a free T-shirt? Keep it. Only cancel newer cards.
Credit mix (10%) The variety of types of credit accounts.	It's actually good for your credit to have a few credit cards, a mortgage, and other loans.
New credit and hard inquiries (10%) Recently opened lines of credit and hard inquiries checking your credit.	Never get a store credit card (they do a hard inquiry), and definitely don't get one when you're about to buy or refinance a home.

Part III
SPEND LESS

11

Spend by Day, Save by MONTH (You Do Not Need a Budget)

When I was in my mid-twenties my dad called and said, "Hey, Kyle, are you still getting the *New York Times*?"

"What are you talking about, Dad?"

I was really confused. I hadn't read the *New York Times* in years — not since my first year of college.

"We were going through all our credit card bills and kept seeing a monthly charge for the *New York Times*," my dad said. "We're trying to cancel this card, so we haven't been buying anything on it. But we have this recurring charge for the *New York Times* on the card that's in your name."

"Dad, that subscription was from my first year of college. That was *seven years ago*. Are you telling me that the *New York Times* has been charging you every month to deliver a newspaper to a dorm room I moved out of seven years ago?"

"I guess so," my dad said. "So this means it's okay to cancel it?"

* * *

Most personal finance books tell you to track every penny of spending. Literally every penny. This is a worthy exercise, and I won't bad-mouth it. If you're inclined to go this route, definitely do it. You will learn a lot. I recommend using a website or app like Mint, which can pull data from all of your credit cards and make pie charts to show you where your money went.

If (like me) you're already conscious of not wasting money and you don't want to track every penny, I have good news — you don't have to. The point of tracking your spending is to find out where you can save money. Let's jump straight to that.

And let me tell you a shortcut: spend by day, save by month.

Recurring monthly charges are what kills everyone's budget more than anything else. Okay, maybe not everyone. If, for instance, you eat caviar every day, or you like to spend your free time juggling Fabergé eggs, that will drain your bank account awfully quickly. But if your guilty pleasure is anything else, then you're probably spending more on your cable bill.

Here is a simple task. You don't need a spreadsheet or even a computer to do it. Just grab a piece of paper and a pen and write down ALL of your monthly or yearly expenses. Every single one.

You need to include yearly expenses because some things (like insurance payments) may only be charged once or twice a year. For any expenses like that, divide that amount to get your monthly payment.

Your list likely includes some or all of the following:

- House payment(s)
    - Mortgage
    - Property taxes
    - Homeowners' insurance premiums
- Car payment(s)
- Auto insurance premiums
- Public transportation passes
- Health insurance premiums
- Life insurance premiums
- Student loan payment(s)
- Childcare
- Utility bills
    - Electric, gas, telephone, cell phone, internet, water, sewer, cable, etc.
- Trash and recycling service
- Cleaning service
- Lawn care
- Snowplowing service
- Subscriptions
    - Magazines, apps, websites, Netflix, Hulu, Disney Plus, etc.
- Financial advisor fees
- Bank fees
- Gym fees
- Credit card annual fees
- Any other debt payments
- Any other recurring charge

This is your target list. Your mission, should you choose to accept it, is to eliminate or decrease as many of these items as possible.

Within parameters, of course. Obviously, do not sell your car if that's the only way to get to work. Look at your list and figure out where you can save. You will know far better than I will. Below are some ideas to help you brainstorm. Take them or leave them.

Downsize your home

See the earlier discussion in Part I of this book about why downsizing your home is the single best thing you can do for your finances and the environment.

Eliminate your housing cost entirely

Consider some more radical ideas for how to lower your monthly home expenditures. Many people pay 25% to 30% (or even more) of their after-tax income on homeownership or rent. Imagine how quickly you could retire if you were to take that same amount of money and invest it?

No, I'm not suggesting you go homeless or live out of your car. But you may want to think about these three possibilities: (1) moving in with your parents, (2) taking on roommates that pay rent to cover your mortgage for you, or (3) buying a multi-unit home and having your renters pay your mortgage for you.

None of these options is easy, particularly if you've got a growing family. But do you know what's even harder? Eating cat food during retirement because you can't afford anything else.

Everything is a trade-off. Given how much money most people spend on housing, you'll want to think about whether you can eliminate this expense.

Insulate your house

Wherever you live, you almost certainly spend money heating your home in the winter, cooling your home in the summer, or (for most of us) doing both. The amount you spend can vary wildly.

Insulation is the largest factor in how much it costs to heat or cool your home. The other major factor is the type of fuel that is being used, but a well-insulated home is relatively inexpensive to heat or cool even when fuel and electricity prices are high.

Insulation is a great investment because it usually pays for itself in just a few years. For instance, if you spend $5,000 buttoning up leaky parts of your house, you would likely save that same amount of money or more in fuel and electricity within just a few years.

And you'll keep saving money every year after that! This is a far greater return on investment than you'll get from any stock or bond purchase.

As a bonus, many states offer incentives for weatherizing your home. This can cut the cost of weatherization drastically and make these investments all the more worthwhile.

Radically lower your energy bill

There are many other ways to radically lower your energy bill. I'll mention four of them: (1) replacing your lightbulbs, (2) getting a smaller (and energy-efficient) refrigerator, (3) using a smart thermostat, and (4) buying or leasing solar panels.

First, replace your lightbulbs. Every single one. About a month or two after my partner and I bought our first house, we changed out all of the lightbulbs. We took out perfectly functional incandescent bulbs and replaced them with light-emitting diode (LED) bulbs. We even replaced rarely used lightbulbs, like the floodlight on the barn and the lights on the hood above our oven. (See what I mean by every single one?)

All told, it cost us about $200. Granted, that was because LED bulbs are heavily subsidized in Vermont due to Vermont's energy efficiency programs. But many other states provide similar subsidies. And even if you have to pay more for LED bulbs, it won't cost you too much, and this is one of the best investments you can make.

When we got our next electric bill, I couldn't believe my eyes. It was practically cut in half. We got our $200 back in about six months, and have saved hundreds, if not thousands, of dollars since then.

Quick side note: make sure to get LED bulbs, not compact fluorescent light (CFL) bulbs. While CFL bulbs are also energy efficient, they, unfortunately, contain mercury. As my brother once told me when he was explaining why he never buys CFL lights, you don't want to worry that when you drop a lightbulb on the floor you've just created a mini hazardous waste site.

Second, get a smaller energy-efficient refrigerator. Yes, you read that right. I know this one is a hard sell in an age when "bigger is better." But let me tell you why you should consider buying a smaller refrigerator.

When we bought a house seven years ago, I noticed that our refrigerator was around 10 years old. It was also smaller than we would have liked — only about 16.5 cubic square feet. I knew that modern refrigerators were much more energy efficient, so I looked into getting a larger energy-efficient refrigerator. The search was much harder than I expected. It turns out that, even with increased efficiency, it is difficult to lower your energy use when you increase the size of your fridge. And, likewise, it's easy to save on your energy bill by getting a smaller fridge.

The best of both worlds is a small, energy-efficient fridge. And, no, I'm not talking about mini-fridges or dorm fridges. I'm just suggesting that it is unlikely you need more than 20 cubic feet, no matter how big your family is. As a bonus, when you have a smaller fridge, you have to be more conscious of what you put in it and will be a lot less likely to waste food (and money) by letting leftovers turn into science experiments.

Third, if you use electric heating or cooling, then get a smart thermostat. It will pay for itself in the first year. A smart thermostat lets you change your home's temperature from anywhere and lets you set your home heating and cooling systems to automatically save energy during the day when no one is there.

Fourth, if you own your home and plan to stay there for many years, look into your state's incentives for getting solar panels and see if it would save you money. Depending on your electric bill and what incentives are available for using solar power, you may find that a solar installation pays for itself within a few years and then saves you money on your power bill every year after that.

Get rid of (or at least lower) monthly and yearly subscriptions

Some subscription services are well worth the price. But most subscription services and pay-by-the-month plans target a particular group of people: those who cannot do math.

You know how to do math. But even you, like all of us, have likely signed up to pay for at least one monthly subscription or plan that is not worth it. I know I have. Now is when that stops.

What's great is that it's never been easier to cancel monthly subscriptions. If you use a free money-tracking service like Mint, it now has a feature that will show you your subscriptions all in one place. Another app to consider is Trim, which specializes in helping you get rid of and lower any monthly recurring charges.

Bike, walk, use public transportation, or rideshare to work, or work from home

Cars cost way more money than we realize. We all know that new cars cost at least a few thousand dollars up front to cover the down payment, taxes, and fees. And then there's the enormous monthly payment.

But we sometimes forget or minimize all the other expenses of having a car: insurance, gas, maintenance, snow tires (if you're in a cold climate), tire changes and rotations, and, of course, the occasional whopper when something needs repair. And is it just me, or do repairs suddenly cost thousands when they used to be hundreds? Just about everything in a new car is a computer now, and unexpected costs can add up quickly.

All told, recent studies show that every car you own costs, on average, more than $750 per month. That's over $9,000 per year! If you can bike, walk, use public transportation, or rideshare to work — or if you can telework from home — you can avoid all these costs.

And note that this is a per-car cost. So if you're in a two-car family, you could potentially save $18,000 if you live close enough to everywhere you need to go and can get by with just renting a car the few times you need one.

It wouldn't be easy, but it's worth considering for $18,000 per year! A more practical option may be to save $9,000 by going down to one car.

Imagine having an extra $9,000 every year to invest.

Get a used electric vehicle or a gas vehicle that gets great mileage

If you need to have a car, you should look for a used electric vehicle or at least a gas car that gets great mileage. No matter where you live, electricity is cheaper than gas, even when gas prices are as low as they are now. And gas prices are sure to increase again before long.

It's amazing how much money you waste when you drive a gas guzzler. Electric vehicles and cars with great gas mileage not only help the environment, but they help your wallet too.

To maximize the mileage you get out of your vehicle, make sure to keep the tires properly inflated. This helps you get more miles per gallon and also makes your tires last much longer!

And whatever kind of mileage your car gets, you'll obviously save money every time you can figure out how to drive less. Remember my dad's daily trips to get his iced tea? You don't want to be my dad. Save gas, save money, and save the planet.

Stop the lawncare madness

If you pay someone to mow your lawn, you are wasting lots of money. But even if you do it on your own, you're spending more time and money than you realize. Lawnmowing equipment and fuel add up quickly. And if you have a gas mower, your carbon footprint soars every time you use it. (Seriously, these things are massive emitters, even when used only once a week.)

And if you're also spending time and money buying fertilizer for your lawn, well then my guess is you put down this book before the end of Part I. If you care at all about your finances or the environment, do not manicure your lawn.

There are much better options out there. Can we agree the grass on your lawn is really a weed? Grass is not nearly as pretty, and far less useful, than the dandelions that people constantly weed out of their lawns.

Unless you are subject to local requirements to maintain grass on your lawn, consider planting a groundcover that does not require mowing. Herbs are a great option, and having some in your yard can save you trips to the grocery store when you (inevitably) run out of the exact thing you need for a particular recipe. You could also replace your lawn with organic berries. Have you noticed how much those things cost when you have to buy them? The last time I got some at the grocery store, I thought the clerk had accidentally rung them up as caviar.

Use the library

Alright, it's time for another dad story. This one is from when I was around 10 years old. My dad and I were in a bookstore and I asked him if I could get a book. His response was: "You can always get whatever books you want."

This is classic Dad. An open-ended offer to one of his kids to get any books they ever want. His statement had a profound impact on me. This was my dad's way of saying that books are important. He's right.

My partner and I tell our kids the same thing — that they can get whatever books they want. Okay, maybe we would add the phrase "age-appropriate" in there.

But here's the difference — we always check the local library first! Yes, you might have to wait a few weeks, or sometimes even a few months. Just think of this as training yourself (and your kids) to enjoy delayed gratification.

With the ease of online book reservations and interlibrary loans, you can get nearly any book in nearly any format for free. The "any format" part is key for me, as I listen to lots of audiobooks. I remember sheepishly asking a librarian if you can use interlibrary loans for audiobooks and being happily surprised to hear that of course you can.

So how much money can you save by using the library? Even if you read just one book per month, getting that book from the library saves you around $100 every year compared to buying those books used and paying for shipping. If you would have bought those books in hardcover, then the savings are even greater. Oh, and by the way, unless you're getting someone a gift or buying a book you plan to reread (like this one!), don't buy hardcovers. When you're only going to read a book once, a hardcover is like premium gas, which my brother likes to refer to as a stupid tax.

My family is well aware of how much I oppose buying hardcover books and how much I love libraries. When I was in law school, the Ann Arbor library would special order hardcover books as soon as they came out. When one of my favorite authors released the latest book in a series that both my dad and I read,

I borrowed it. This was right before winter break. After I finished reading it, I brought it to Vermont with me, wrapped it up, and gave it to my dad for Christmas! When he opened it, I explained that I would need it back a week later when I returned to Ann Arbor. He finished it within two days (as he usually does), so it worked out great! Of course, my family never misses an opportunity to tease me about the time I gave my dad a library book for Christmas.

The biggest cost savings from libraries comes from audiobooks. Going back to the example of reading one book a month, if you buy a single audiobook every month (or subscribe to a monthly audiobook service like Audible), you might end up paying $200 every year. With the library, it would be free. Over five years, this adds up to $1,000. Now we're talking big numbers.

Speaking of $1,000 for audiobooks, let me tell you a quick story about the time I once nearly lost $1,000 on the purchase of a single audiobook. If this story doesn't convince you to use your local library, I don't know what will.

What happened was that I had read a review of a great audiobook and saw that it was on sale at Audible for $15. When I clicked "purchase," I was expecting to be directed to a webpage where I would enter my payment information. Instead, because I had apparently at one point set up "one-click purchasing," Audible immediately tried to charge the credit card that I had given it many years earlier.

Thankfully, the purchase failed because I had recently canceled that card. The reason I canceled it was that the company had tried to raise the interest rate on the card from 4.9% to over 20%. Because this card had a ridiculously low rate of 4.9% (a rate that only existed for the briefest of times), I had accumulated a balance on that card during law school. After all, this rate was even lower than the 7.9% rate on my student loans. (Let me emphasize that this is the only time I ever carried a balance on a credit card, and I would never recommend anyone do it, even if the rate is just 4.9%.)

Long story short, when the credit card company tried to raise the interest rate on me, I canceled the card so that I could keep the 4.9% rate while I paid off the balance. In the cancelation process, I thankfully asked lots of questions. I learned that my card (and the soaring new 20% interest rate) would be "reactivated" if I made any charges on it. What? I told them I didn't want that to happen. They eventually told me that they could assign a new number to the account to make sure that I never accidentally used the card and thus incurred a permanent increased interest rate on the balance. I asked them to do that.

My extra caution paid off when, a few months later, Audible tried to charge the canceled card. Had that charge gone through, my interest rate would have skyrocketed. When I later calculated how bad it would have been, I realized that I came awfully close to losing around $1,000 in interest! This is yet another reason to always use the library.

Don't buy new furniture

When I was in college, I think I accidentally helped someone steal a couch. I say "think" because I honestly don't know whether he had permission to take this couch or not.

This friend was an eccentric character, and he asked me to help him go get a couch one day. I hopped in his sport utility vehicle and we drove to our school's fraternity row. He pulled up to the back of a building and told me to "just play along." I tried to ask him what he meant, but he was already walking ahead of me and didn't respond.

I followed him up to a large couch where someone was seated.

"We're grabbing this couch," my friend said.

With a puzzled look, the other person slowly got up and moved to another couch — a matching one with the same pattern as the one we were taking. My friend and I then grabbed opposite sides of the now-abandoned couch and walked it outside, slid it into the back of his sport utility vehicle, and drove off.

I was confused, to say the least, particularly since we had left with just one of a matching set of couches. I couldn't imagine why the fraternity would have sold just one of a two-part set of couches. My friend then refused to answer any questions about whether he had permission to take the couch, which of course just made me all the more suspicious. But at that point, the deed was done, and I didn't see any way I'd convince my friend to give back the couch.

Please note that this is not a recommended way of getting furniture. Not only could this have landed my friend — and possibly me — in jail (although I maintain that I'm innocent because I was duped into being his accomplice), but it also could have gone even worse. My friend and I were not a part of the fraternity community. We were ultimate frisbee players. We're lucky we made it out of there without receiving bodily harm!

So please do not steal furniture.

But don't buy it either! At least not new. Okay, most people prefer to buy mattresses new, and that makes sense. For everything else, furniture is incredibly expensive, and you're guaranteed to ruin it eventually.

Between yard sales, thrift stores, craigslist, the Facebook marketplace, and any friends who are moving, you should be able to piece together whatever furniture you need for your home. It doesn't have to be pretty. It just needs to be functional.

12

PLAN YOUR MEALS AND SNACKS

I f you take care of your monthly expenses, then you may not have to worry about daily expenses. But don't go too crazy here.

When I was in high school, I went to the grocery store with my dad. When we were picking out orange juice, my dad grabbed a half-gallon that cost $9.

"Dad, I don't think we need $9 orange juice," I told him.

"Always get the best you can afford," he replied.

By now, I don't have to tell you how terrible this advice was.

And my dad applied this same philosophy to many of his purchases. For instance, when the first iPod Touch came out, he bought one right away. A few months later, my family went out for dinner. We got into a debate over something, and I asked my dad for his iPod Touch so we could Google the answer.

As I signed on to the restaurant's free Wi-Fi network and fired up Google, my dad looked over my shoulder and said, "You can get the internet on that?"

"Yes, Dad, that's the whole point," I said. "That, and storing music and podcasts."

"You can put music on it?" he asked.

"Dad, what do you think this is for?"

"It's got my calendar on it," he said.

Yes, my dad had bought an iPod Touch for the calendar. Not only that, but he had bought the most expensive version of the iPod Touch. Instead of paying $300 for the 8GB version, he had paid $500 for the 32GB version. When I checked his settings, I saw that he was using less than 2GB of memory, and I don't think he ever used any more than that.

So whether it's orange juice, electronics, or anything else, I don't recommend my dad's philosophy of buying the best you can afford.

But I'm also not a fan of self-deprivation or "spending freezes." Remember that your big savings are going to be on your monthly expenses. As long as you're keeping your monthly expenses in check, you don't need to stress out about smaller daily and one-time purchases.

If you want to go out for drinks with co-workers, go for it. If you need new work clothes, get them. Don't deprive yourself of these things to save money.

Instead, be mindful of how much you spend on meeting these needs and wants. In other words, unlike my dad, aim to find the least expensive way to get what you want. And if you do this right, you'll find that you don't even have to sacrifice quality. You won't be depriving yourself in any way.

There's a reason why just about every book on personal finance singles out coffee shops as a waste of money. According to David Bach, if you took the money you spent on coffee shops every day and invested it in the stock market, you'd have enough money to own your own island by now.

Okay, he doesn't really say that, but he does claim, with a fair amount of evidence, that daily habits like visiting a coffee shop add up to a lot more money than you think. And coffee shops are such a great example because they specialize in coffee that is overpriced and tastes bad.

At home, you can make good coffee that costs less. First thing every morning, I have a large cup of coffee. I make a second cup to put in a thermos to bring to work. Even using organic coffee grounds, each cup of coffee costs me about a quarter. And it tastes way better than anything I could get at a coffee shop.

Also, coffee shops have a way of getting you to buy more than just a cup of coffee. I read about someone who started tracking her spending and realized that she lost $20 every week buying bottled water at her local coffee shop. That's over $1,000 a year.

Some people really like bottled water. That's fine, but if you have access to clean tap water, you shouldn't ever buy bottled water. Put tap water (or filtered water if necessary) in a water bottle and pop it in the refrigerator. That will give you everything great about bottled water at no cost.

One of the best ways to cut down on your daily expenses is to plan your meals and snacks. When you leave your house for work, or to go on a day trip with your family, you should have all of the food and drinks you'll need until you get back home. This one trick can save you thousands of dollars every year.

When you're planning your meals and snacks, let me mention two more tips for saving thousands of dollars on food.

First, try to eat less meat and dairy. I'm not saying go vegetarian, and I'm certainly not going to say go vegan. I'm from Vermont — a single day rarely goes by without some extra sharp cheddar cheese. But our family has sworn off beef. We eat other meats, but not every day. Instead, we get a lot of our protein from beans, lentils, nuts, and copious amounts of organic peanut butter.

Cutting back on meat and dairy will greatly help your bank account, not to mention your health and your carbon footprint. In fact, what you eat has more of an impact on your carbon footprint than what you drive.

Meat (and beef in particular) is incredibly carbon-intensive. Yes, I'm talking about cow farts here. And burps. No, I'm not joking. The methane from cow gas is a huge contributor to climate change. Additionally, trees (including rainforests) are often chopped down to make room for cattle. That also accelerates climate change. By cutting back on meat and dairy, these minor tweaks to your shopping habits will save you lots of money and make the world a better place.

My second tip for saving money on food is to grow your own fruits and vegetables. If you have any inclination toward gardening, and a place to do it (either at your home or a community garden), you should give it a try. There's nothing better than garden-fresh produce, and growing food on your own will save you lots of money on your grocery bill.

If you end up with lots of homegrown produce, you may need to invest in a chest freezer to store it all. That will allow you to enjoy your fruits and vegetables year-round. Like refrigerators, you'll want to get the smallest one that will meet your needs, and make sure it's energy efficient.

Note that if you end up storing your produce in a freezer, do not ever invite my dad over to your house. My mom learned this the hard way. She's always been into gardening, and when I was growing up, she stored lots of produce in a freezer in our basement. One day she went to the basement to get some green beans and found that everything in the freezer was ruined. It had all thawed and rotted. My mom couldn't believe it. What had happened to the freezer? How did it break? Then she looked at the back of the freezer and found that the electric cord had been unplugged. In its place was the electric cord for my dad's pinball machine.

How my parents' marriage survived that incident, I have no idea.

13

Do Not Eat RAMEN or
Handwash Your Suits

When people discover the 4% Rule and start thinking seriously about financial independence and retiring early, they sometimes go a little too far. Cutting expenses is great — crucial, in fact, if you're serious about getting your financial house in order. No amount of income will ever be enough if you always spend it all. But you don't want to go too far.

There are plenty of stories out there of people cutting expenses in an extreme fashion. I'll give just two examples — one speaking generally, and one that's more personal.

The general caution is that you don't want to save money by eating ramen noodles. They're tasty, they're cheap, and they're a complete meal. But it's not a good idea.

Your health will almost certainly suffer. In fact, the grocery store is generally not the best place to save money. Notice that I said, "the grocery store" — not "food." If you're eating out regularly, then that is a great place to save money.

Cooking at home will save you lots of money. And you'll even find that when you decide to eat out, you'll appreciate it far more. By cooking more at home, you'll save money even when you buy high-quality groceries. If you need fast, easy meals, consider buying an Instant Pot (or two or three) — they're lifesavers and will make a chef out of anyone who likes to eat out.

Our family splurges on organic and local produce, grains, and meat whenever we can. Yes, it's more expensive, but I'm okay with that for two reasons. First, I view the added cost as an investment in our long-term health. Many studies have shown that there are health benefits to organic fruits, vegetables, and whole grains compared to their conventional counterparts. Second, I'm okay paying extra for organic local food because I don't think it really is paying "extra." Rather, those food products are priced correctly. It's everything else that is artificially subsidized through farming and other processes that cause long-term harm to our health and the environment. This is one place where, if I can afford to pay for the more expensive option, I will.

Alright, enough preaching. Now let me tell you a much more personal — and lighter — story about an attempt to save money that didn't exactly pan out for me.

At the beginning of my legal career, I applied to work as a law clerk at the Vermont Supreme Court. When I got an interview, I knew I needed to get my suit dry-cleaned before I showed up at the Court. It did not smell good and I wasn't about to lose my dream clerkship because I showed up smelling like I just got home from the gym.

I called a local dry-cleaner and learned that it would cost $20 to get my suit jacket and pants dry-cleaned.

Twenty dollars? That seemed like an exorbitant sum for such a minor task. I was not about to be taken to the cleaners (so to speak).

I hopped on Google to see how hard it would be to handwash my suit. It couldn't be *that* difficult, right? I quickly found instructions and got to work.

The first step was to fill up the bottom inch of our bathtub. No problem. Then I added soap and did some scrubbing. This was easy!

The next step was to dry the suit. To avoid stretching out the shoulder area of the suit jacket, the instructions warned against using a coat hanger. Instead, it said to lay down a towel on the floor and put the suit jacket on top of it. Done. I moved on to another task while my suit dried. An hour or so later, I came back into the room where I had left it.

"Nemo!!!" I yelled at the top of my lungs. That was the name of our golden retriever.

It was a hot day, and Nemo had decided to cool himself off by laying down on the nice damp suit jacket on the floor.

As I frantically tried to brush the dog hair off with my hand, I smelled the suit jacket to survey the damage. Not surprisingly, it was bad. There's a reason we have a name for "wet-dog smell."

But I figured maybe it would get better once the suit jacket fully dried. Of course, I could forget about laying it back on the floor. I was going to have to risk stretching out the shoulder area. I grabbed a coat hanger and hung it up.

I wish that were the end of the story. But it got even worse.

The place I hung the suit jacket was in a doorway at the edge of our kitchen. Later that night, as I opened the oven to see if my baked fish was ready, I saw the fumes from the oven waft out and pass directly through my suit jacket.

At that point, I wished I had just gone ahead and paid the dry-cleaners $20. (If you're wondering, I did not get the clerkship, although I reapplied the following year and showed up with a professionally dry-cleaned suit. I did get the job that time.)

There are lots more examples of times when you're far better off spending money than trying to save a few dollars. When I received my most recent raise, I decided to splurge by spending $20 on a 12-pack of undershirts. I had been using ones that had become stained, and I figured it was time to turn those into rags and get some new ones.

So yes, find ways to save money, but don't go crazy. If you ever find yourself eating ramen or hand-washing a suit, it's time to take a step back.

Remember that the big savings always happen in your monthly recurring charges. Get the big wins there, and don't worry about occasional splurges in your daily expenses.

14

ALWAYS ASK FOR DISCOUNTS

"**I** made $8,000 today, and so can you."

That's what I wrote on a note to my college roommate during our senior year. It was true. And he did the same thing I had done. I used my money to travel to Asia with my partner. My roommate used his money to buy a fishing boat. I got to go for a ride in it many years later when I visited him in South Carolina.

So how exactly did two college seniors make $8,000 each in one day? What happened was I asked a question. That's it.

My roommate and I were both on full-tuition scholarships at college. My scholarship even covered room, board, and books. To maintain the scholarship, we had to be enrolled as full-time students. I knew that this meant taking at least 12 hours of credits each semester. But as I approached the final semester of my senior year, I didn't need 12 hours of credits to graduate. And I had applied for — and been accepted into — a 20-hour-per-week internship. I wanted to focus on my internship and did not want to take a full course load on top of that.

So I scheduled an appointment with the Dean of Students. My plan was to find out if there was any way I could keep my scholarship if I signed up for only four hours of courses, rather than the minimum of 12 hours.

Expecting the dean to say no, I was happily surprised when he instead said, "No problem."

It turns out the 12-hour minimum didn't apply during the last semester. The rule for the last semester was that you had to take enough credits to meet whatever you needed to graduate.

"In fact," the dean said, "if you take only four hours of credits, you'll get refunded for the other eight credits."

"What?" I asked. I was very confused. The dean knew I was on a scholarship and didn't pay a dime for any of my credits.

"Yes, you get a refund," he said.

He then explained that once the scholarship money was credited to my account, there was no way to return it to the scholarship fund. He assured me that this was perfectly fine and that it sounded like the best choice for me given my options.

I left the dean's office in a state of stupor. It seemed too good to be true. I had gone into his office hoping to get a break on the number of credits I had to take that semester. I left not only with exactly what I wanted but with a completely unexpected $8,000 as well.

I tell this story because it illustrates the importance of asking for what you want. I'm certain that many other students, in the same situation as me, just buckled down and took 12 hours of credits their final semester, even though they didn't need 12 hours to graduate. Some of them were probably doing that on top of a demanding internship. Had they simply paused for a moment and asked for what they wanted, they may have ended up far better off.

Asking for what you want applies across the board. Yet way too few people actually do it. It had never occurred to my roommate to ask about taking fewer than 12 credit hours the last semester. But because I asked the question, we both benefited greatly.

It is amazing how much money people leave on the table because they don't ever ask for what they want. For instance, when something costs more than you think it should, why not ask for a discount?

When you walk into a hotel at ten o'clock at night and ask how much a room costs, do you accept the first answer they give you? If you do, you're leaving money on the table. I worked briefly at a hotel front desk, and I assure you that when it's ten o'clock at night and they still have rooms open, they'll take a lot less than the first number they give you. All it takes is a simple follow-up question of whether they can offer a discount.

Do you need a new appliance? Search around for the best deals (which is easy now that everything's online), but once you find what you want, don't be afraid to go to the store and ask if they can give you a better price. The worst they can say is no. And there's an awfully good chance they'll end up giving you some kind of discount.

For instance, there might be a perfectly good floor model that is marked down 20% from what a new model costs. Or an open-box item that has a similar discount. Or they might tell you that there's no discount now, but that if you wait another few weeks, there will be a big sale. Keep asking. See if they can give you that sale price now. They have a lot more leeway on prices than you might think.

Your monthly bills are another place where you can save a lot by asking for discounts. Do you believe your internet company when it tells you that a promotional rate is only available for one year? Call them up at the end of that year and tell them that if the price increases, you'll need to look into getting service from another company. They'll almost certainly offer a better price.

Even consumer debt like credit cards can be negotiated. It is, of course, far better to never incur this debt in the first place. But if you do, you may be able to work out a deal with your credit card company to repay only a portion of what you owe. The same goes for medical debt like hospital expenses. They may be willing to consider your bill paid in full even if you can only pay a portion of it. Unfortunately, when you negotiate over a debt you already owe, you run the risk of hurting your credit score. You may also owe taxes on any amount that is forgiven. So make sure you know all the consequences if you take this route.

One more thing before I close this chapter on asking for discounts. It's a quote from Paula Pant, who has an excellent podcast called *Afford Anything* (and also regularly appears on another wonderful podcast called *Stacking Benjamins*). She notes that discounts are great, but "you can save 100% by not buying it."

15

Buy USED (Except for Wedding Rings and Running Shoes)

'll be the first to admit that it's really hard to buy a used car when you have the money to buy a new one. In fact, my partner and I both currently drive cars that we got new. My only excuse is the same one Ted Turner gives when he talks about the problems of overpopulation. Whenever he raises that subject, people call him a hypocrite since he has five kids. His response is always the same: "I didn't know all this back when I had them. And it's not like I can get rid of them now!"

My partner and I are also stuck with our cars. But now that I know the numbers better, I can't see us buying a new car again. They simply depreciate way too quickly.

Yes, it's more work to buy a used car. Yes, it feels riskier because you don't know if it's in good shape. (Pro tip: check the dipstick and make sure that the end of it is not burned.) But you're always way better off buying used than new.

This goes for just about anything, not just cars. Books, electronics, furniture, clothes. You can find a used version of nearly everything online or at a thrift shop for much cheaper than what you'd pay if you bought it new.

Yes, there are some exceptions, like engagement and wedding rings. Unless it's a family heirloom, your spouse does not want a used ring. If you've done a good job selecting your spouse, you shouldn't need to spend too much on a ring, but do buy something new.

Another thing you always want to buy new is running shoes. This is a matter of health, as used shoes do not provide the cushioning that you need for regular running. Your knees and back will thank you.

I'm sure there are other exceptions too, but your default should always be to buy used.

Buying used is not only good for your wallet — it helps the planet too. It's much more wasteful to throw things out and replace them with something new. When you buy used, you're reusing something that would otherwise go to waste.

16

Get ENTERTAINED for Free

No, this chapter is not about how you can share a Netflix account with a friend or relative. This is not about how you can do the same thing with Prime Video, Hulu, Disney Plus, HBO, and every other streaming service.

Yes, I happen to know that this works. And, yes, I may be the beneficiary of having a dad who, of course, subscribes to all of these services. (He's never met a monthly charge he didn't like!) But everyone already knows (and does) this.

This chapter is about other ways you can get entertained for free. I'm talking about live entertainment, like shows, concerts, and plays. And other activities outside of your home, like zoos and museums. My family regularly makes use of the following three ways of getting free entertainment: (1) finding free shows, (2) ushering, and (3) using library passes.

Find free shows

It's amazing how many free shows happen every day if you look for them. In the summer, most places have free outdoor concerts on a regular basis. And no, it's not just the neighborhood kids trying out a new grunge-emo-techno fusion. Real musicians are giving free concerts.

And dance shows. And even plays. Look online or in a local magazine to see what free venues are happening. And focus on outdoor events, as free indoor events usually expect you to buy food. At the outdoor events, they'll have food available (they've got to make money somehow), but you can easily bring your own as well.

Usher

Imagine being in the front row of a theatre while the real Professor X (or Captain Picard for you *Star Trek* fans) stands less than five feet in front of you and delivers a soliloquy from *The Tempest*. He's so close that you could lean forward and touch him.

Imagine watching Bobby McFerrin live in concert — not once, but twice. And imagine that on one of those nights, he comes right up to you and your father-in-law as you stand at the side of the theatre. He moves the mic toward you to see if he can get you to repeat the rhythm he just sang. You lean back and hope he skips by you and goes to your father-in-law instead. It works. And when your father-in-law gets the mic, he decides to ignore Bobby McFerrin's rhythm and instead improvise his own beatbox. It's over-the-top and the audience erupts in laughter. Bobby McFerrin laughs too.

These are real experiences. And I didn't pay a dime for them. I've seen many other incredible shows for free as well. All by offering to be a volunteer usher. You know those folks who take your tickets and show you to your seats? They're usually volunteers. It's easy work, takes less than an hour, and you get to stay and watch the show for free afterward.

It's a great gig. If this interests you, then call or email your local theatres, including any nearby college campuses, and find out the process for becoming a volunteer usher.

Use library passes

Another free way to get entertained is to pick up passes to zoos and museums from your local library. Most people don't know that libraries provide this service. Call or email your library and find out whether they provide free passes. You might have to wait a few weeks to get one, but this can save you a lot of money.

17

FIX IT AND DO IT YOURSELF (IF YOU CAN)

"**Y**ou got a new TV, Dad?" I asked as I entered my parents' basement.
"Yeah, the old one broke," he said.
"I thought you just bought that one," I said.
"Well, it wasn't working, so I gave it to our neighbor."
Makes sense. If something isn't working, you buy a replacement.

The only thing is that it turned out that the reason my dad's TV wasn't working was that it had been unplugged. We learned this from our neighbor. He was happy to discover that he had received a TV that worked perfectly well, so long as you plugged it in.

Now I'll be the first to admit that the apple does not fall far from the tree. I would have known to plug in a TV before deciding that it was broken, but that's about the extent of my handiness.

Still, even I'm not completely inept. In fact, I recently saved our family $75 on a DIY project that took less than an hour.

The $75 savings came when we needed to have our septic tank pumped. We live in a rural area where we have our own septic tank and leach field. If you're from the city, you might not have ever heard of a leach field. I'm jealous. Every three or four years, the septic tank needs to be pumped. No, I did not do the pumping myself. Ick. Double ick. That is something you should never, ever, ever DIY.

What I did do is dig up the soil above the septic tank. The spot was easy to find because the last time I dug it up, I did it wrong and the grass never regrew. (Hmmm, maybe I shouldn't have done this on my own?) So when I saw the dead grass, I knew exactly where to dig. It took me no time to remove about six inches of soil in a 2-foot-by-2-foot area. This small amount of work saved us $75 on our bill for the septic tank pumping. For that hourly rate, I'll dig holes any day. And we've come to love that little dead patch in our yard.

Another job I do myself every year — for an even higher hourly rate — is sweeping our chimney. If we pay someone to do this, it costs as much as $200 each time. Instead, I bought a chimney brush for $20, and I borrow long poles from my neighbor, who also sweeps his chimney. The entire process takes about half an hour.

We also installed a new toilet at our house. We know an amazing plumber, but he charges at least $150 for every visit, no matter how simple the job. A friend of ours offered to help us install our new toilet, and we took him up on it. Turns out, it's not exactly rocket science. It's quite straightforward. We did just fine and saved lots of money.

These are just a few examples of projects that you can do yourself at significant savings compared to hiring someone else.

There are, of course, limits on what you should try to do yourself. For instance, I only sweep my own chimney because I can reach it safely without risking a fall. And I would never try to install a dishwasher myself. There are just too many things that could go wrong, and I'd be worried every time I ran the dishwasher that a hose would spring loose and I would witness a kitchen tsunami. My father-in-law, on the other hand, felt comfortable installing a dishwasher and recently did this himself, with a little help from my partner. Did I mention that she is the handy one among us?

Figure out your comfort level for fix-it projects, and don't be afraid to hop on Google or YouTube and see if you can learn how to fix things yourself. There are times when you need a professional. But most of the time, Google and YouTube will suffice. Especially if you have your partner do it.

18

BE SMART ABOUT SCHOLARSHIPS
AND STUDENT LOANS

Most personal finance books go on and on about how you should think twice before you go to college. They note how expensive college has become and that many great jobs do not require a college degree. They then say that if you're going to go to college, go to the cheapest school you can.

I have a different point of view. Yes, college is not for everyone. Yes, you want to look at how much it costs and take that into account. For instance, if a school specializes in a particular program that you are interested in, and it costs less than a higher-ranked school, you probably want to save your money rather than chase rankings. But, in my mind, money should never be what drives your decision about whether to attend college and, if so, what kind of college experience you have.

You know this already. If one of your kids gets into Harvard, are you going to sit them down at the dinner table and ask whether they really need to go to college? Are you going to take out brochures from the local community college and pressure them to go there because it's cheaper? Not likely.

Now you may remember the story about my dad declining a full scholarship at Princeton so that he could go to Harvard. If you now think my dad made the right choice there, let me disabuse you of the notion that my dad ever makes the right choice when it comes to financial matters. He had a full scholarship to *Princeton*. That is every bit as good a school as Harvard.

When you're choosing between equally good schools, then yes, go with the cheaper option! But you should never choose a worse educational experience just to save money.

In my opinion, and I know this departs from the conventional financial advice that most others give, people should usually go to the best school that accepts them. That is going to provide them with the best education, the best life experiences, the best alumni network, and the most options going forward for the rest of their life. You simply cannot put a price tag on any of that.

Of course, there is a price tag — and a big one at that!

So who should pay for your kids to attend college — you or them? I have two answers to this question.

First, look for another option altogether: scholarships. If your kid wants to go to college, the best option is obviously a full scholarship. I'll discuss this in more detail below.

My second answer is that, if someone has to pay, consider talking to your kids about them paying. Really. This does not have to be on you. That's clearly the case if you don't have any kids. And for those of us with kids, I don't know when or why the personal finance community decided that it's up to us to pay for our kids' college. I love our kids more than anything in the world. But I don't see why my partner and I should pay for their college.

I don't see why our kids should have to pay either. Most developed nations extend free education beyond high school and cover college as well. Although it's always difficult to predict what American politicians might do, there's a clear trend toward greater governmental support for post-secondary education. If that trend continues, then we may never need to worry about paying for our kids going to college. Alternatively, if you've ever thought about living in another country, you may be able to move somewhere that already offers free college education for your kids.

If you have lots of money to spare, then paying for your kids to go to college is wonderful. There are far worse uses of your money. When you tell your kids that you'll pay for their education, it gives them leeway to pursue their passions, regardless of cost. And it tells them how important education is. This is an amazing gift. If you're in the position to do this, then by all means do so.

But for most of us, we simply do not have the money to create college funds for our kids. I'm writing this chapter to reassure you that this is okay. Just like the internet and smartphones, our kids will figure it out — and probably do a better job of it than we ever could.

Going to college is as good a time as any to show our kids that there's no free lunch. The world consists of trade-offs. In fact, these conversations should start long before your kids go to college. Let them know in high school that they'll be on their own, and talk through some of the options they'll have to save money during college.

Let me mention four money-saving options that everyone should consider when it comes to paying for college: (1) taking Advanced Placement (AP) courses and tests during high school, (2) applying for scholarships, (3) minimizing living expenses during college, and (4) being smart about student loans.

Encourage them to take AP courses and tests

At the end of my first year of college, I learned that one of my classmates was going to be a junior the next year.

"How's that?" I asked him.

He explained that he had taken eight AP tests during his senior year of high school and had scored high enough on them to come into college with a full year's worth of credits.

"Wow," I said. "My high school only offered a couple of AP courses."

"Mine too," he replied. "I just picked up some books on other topics, studied them, and then took the AP tests."

This was some seriously impressive out-of-the-box thinking. He had spent a few weeks studying hard while most of his high-school classmates were already checked out. His reward? Easily completing college in three years, rather than four, which saved him around $50,000 in tuition, room, and board. This is probably the highest hourly wage a high schooler can ever make.

Look far and wide for scholarships

There are lots of scholarships out there. They take some work, but maximizing scholarships is the best way to save money on college. Although I only applied to three colleges, which is not recommended (I only did this because I needed to be somewhere that I could compete in whitewater kayaking), I also applied for several scholarships. One of them worked out, and my scholarship paid for my entire college education, including expenses. As I noted in an earlier chapter, I actually ended up profiting from the scholarship I received.

When I decided to get a master's degree and then a law degree, I was not as successful in getting scholarships. I had to pay full freight for my master's degree. My law school provided a $7,000 per year scholarship. That helped, but it was just a drop in the bucket. As a result, between my master's degree and three years of law school, I racked up $200,000 in student loans. And the number only went up from there, as my payments on student loans were income-based and often did not even cover the interest. This meant that even when I made payments on my student loans, the amount I owed kept increasing. Thankfully, as discussed in more detail below, I made sure that I qualified for a loan forgiveness program so that I didn't have to pay these loans myself.

There are lots of great resources out there (websites and entire books) on how to apply for — and win — scholarships. If you or your kids are going to college anytime soon, you'll want to put some serious research into finding out all of the available scholarships and making sure you give them your best shot.

Minimize living expenses

Yes, college tuition is outrageous. This fact became all the more obvious during the 2020 coronavirus pandemic when the following meme started making the rounds:

Annual Streaming Price

	$108
	$72
You Tube Red	$120
	$132
	$84
HARVARD UNIVERSITY	$50,420

To make matters worse, tuition is not the only thing you pay for when you go to college. Living expenses also add up quickly. Fortunately, this is one place that you can save big time. To avoid drowning in student loans, you should find ways to minimize living expenses during college.

Your biggest living expense, by far, is housing. This is true whether you're living in a dorm or renting an apartment. One option to consider is living at home or with other relatives while you go to college. If you can do that for free, or for a small amount of rent, you'll save lots of money.

Another option to consider is house hacking. This is the concept we discussed in an earlier chapter. It involves buying a house that has multiple units (or at least multiple bedrooms) and then renting out those extra units and bedrooms. This can significantly decrease your housing expenses and may even provide you with another stream of income.

Be smart about student loans

So once you've gone to school and taken on anywhere from a few thousand dollars to a few hundred thousand dollars in student loans, how do you manage to pay off those loans? Let me mention three things you want to make sure you consider as you work on paying off student loans: (1) the tax deduction for student loan interest, (2) the benefits of federal loans (including loan forgiveness options), and (3) the benefits of refinancing student loans.

First, if you're paying student loans, make sure you take advantage of the tax deduction. As of 2021, as long as you're within certain income limits, you can deduct up to $2,500 in interest incurred on student loans. Depending on your tax bracket and the state you live in, this will save you anywhere from a few hundred to around a thousand dollars when you do your taxes. Of course, you'd be far better off not incurring that interest in the first place, but if you're stuck with student loans, then you might as well get the tax benefit.

Note that you should take this tax benefit into account when you have extra money that you want to put towards paying off your debt. So, for instance, if you inherit $20,000, and you want to use it to either pay off a car loan that has a 5%

interest rate or your student loans that have a 6% interest rate, you may be better off paying the car loan. Here's the math on this: if you pay off the car, then you'll pay $1,200 in interest (6% of $20,000) on your student loans the next year. This seems like a bad deal because if you instead used the $20,000 to pay off your student loans, your car payment would have incurred only $1,000 in interest (5% of $20,000). So why pay the extra $200? Because by keeping the $20,000 in student loans, you get a tax deduction on the $1,200 you paid in interest. Depending on your tax bracket, this almost certainly saves you more than $200. And it would continue to save you money every year after that.

The second thing to keep in mind with student loans is that federal student loans carry significant benefits. For instance, during 2020 and 2021, the CARES Act and later Executive Orders and relief bills suspended federal student loan payments, and the suspension applied to any interest that might have otherwise accrued. This benefit was not available for private student loans.

Another significant benefit of federal student loans is that you can put them on an income-driven repayment plan. This allows your monthly payment to ebb and flow with your income, making those monthly payments much more manageable. And if you ever need to defer payments on your loans altogether (for instance, due to medical reasons), that's generally going to be easier to do when it comes to federal loans, as opposed to private loans.

Also, the federal government may end up providing additional benefits for those who have federal student loans. We never know what Congress will do, but in recent years there has been serious talk about forgiving federal student loans (or at least a portion of them). I also would not be surprised if a future Congress decides to drastically lower the interest rate on these loans. You should keep these benefits in mind if you're ever thinking about refinancing your student loans, as you may not want to lose out on the benefits of federal loans.

Speaking of the benefits of federal loans, there's one that reigns supreme: loan forgiveness. In particular, there are two ways you can get your federal student loans discharged entirely. (Okay, there are three ways, since your student loans get discharged if you die, but I don't recommend that. Nor should you consider bankruptcy, since not even that will get your student loans discharged.)

One way to have your federal loans forgiven is to make 25 years of payments on an income-driven repayment plan. At the end of those 25 years, whatever you still owe on your federal student loans is wiped out entirely.

Now there are two important caveats. One is that very few people still owe money on their student loans after 25 years. You would have to have taken out a lot in loans and maintained a relatively low income to make this option work. The second caveat is that at the end of the 25 years, the amount forgiven is likely going to be treated as taxable income. So you'd need to be ready for a really big tax bill.

The second — and much better way — to have your federal student loans forgiven is to spend 10 years working in government or at a not-for-profit organization. This is the Public Service Loan Forgiveness program. It rocks. Not only can you get tens to hundreds of thousands of dollars forgiven entirely, but it is now well established that this type of loan forgiveness is tax free!

Now if you think you might be eligible for this program, you'll want to do your homework and make sure you dot all your I's and cross all your T's. For instance, you'll need to make sure your loans are all in the right type of repayment plan and that your employer qualifies. There are lots of horror stories out there about people who thought they were on track for loan forgiveness, only to be denied at the end of their 10 years. But if you do things right, this program really works.

How do I know it works? I've done it myself!

I've spent my entire career in state government. After putting in the required number of years and payments, I recently had over $230,000 in federal loans wiped out entirely! It was a long journey, and I was so relieved that I cried when it finally happened. Here's the before and after:

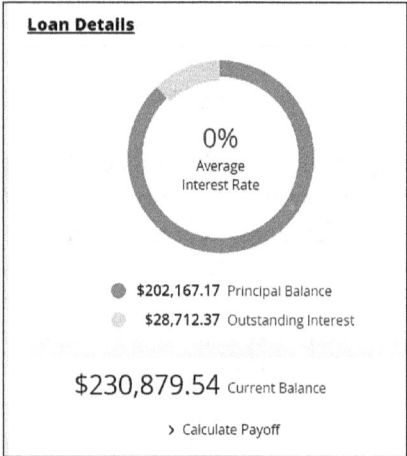

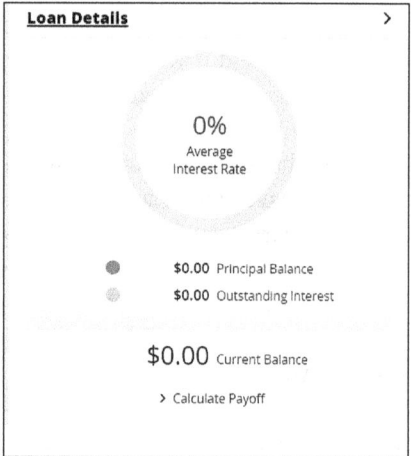

A co-worker of mine got a similar amount of student loans forgiven last year. The program really does work. And the best part is that, unlike many other forms of loan forgiveness, Public Service Loan Forgiveness is tax-free. The Department of Education even sends a letter confirming that all loans have been forgiven, that the remaining balance is $0, and that there are no taxes due.

The last thing I'll mention on student loans is refinancing. For all the reasons we just discussed, please do not even think about refinancing your federal student loans if there's any chance you're going to get those loans forgiven through a program like Public Service Loan Forgiveness. The moment you refinance federal student loans with a private lender, they're no longer federal loans, and you've lost all of the benefits that go along with federal loans.

Private student loans, on the other hand, don't have the benefits of federal loans. For private student loans, you just want to make sure you get the lowest interest rate possible.

In 2020, these interest rates plummeted. This means that if you haven't yet looked into refinancing your private student loans, now is the time.

Here's how it worked for me. In early 2020, I had around $30,000 in private student loans and was making a monthly payment of $270. I called my lender to find out how many more years of payments I had left on these loans. The answer was a whopping 20 years.

This meant that I would end up paying nearly $65,000 over those 20 years — more than double what I owed. After some internet research, I found a 4% fixed interest rate for a 10-year loan. The monthly payment was only $300. In other words, by refinancing and paying an extra $30 per month, I knocked off 10 years of payments! And I'm saving nearly $30,000 in interest.

As with any refinancing, you'll need to do your research and read the fine print to make sure there are not any hidden fees. But this type of research is easier than ever these days. And the great thing about refinancing student loans is that you usually do not have to pay anything upfront. When you refinance a home, you often incur thousands of dollars in closing costs. Not so for student loans. Most of the major lenders do not charge fees for refinancing student loans. This means you can focus on which lender offers the lowest interest rate. And it also means you should continually keep an eye out for even lower rates, as you may want to consider another refinancing whenever interest rates drop.

19

GET HITCHED FOR LESS

"**D**o I need a $10,000 dress, or can I get away with a $5,000 one?"

My brother claims to have seen an article with a headline like that. Whether this article actually exists, I don't know, but it exemplifies what most people experience when they decide to get married. The numbers are truly astounding. For instance, a website called The Knot did a survey in 2019 and found that the average cost of a wedding is $33,900.

Many people spend even more on a wedding, and there's no shame at all in that. Every wedding involves incredibly personal decisions at every turn. So much so that I hesitated to say anything about weddings in this book. In the end, I decided to include this chapter simply as an illustration that it is possible to get married without going into debt if you choose to do so.

My dad wore Crocs to my wedding.

To be fair, I did too. And so did my partner and all eight members of the wedding party.

It was a very laid-back affair. My partner and I decided that our outfits and those of the wedding party would form a rainbow to symbolize our support for those couples who were not allowed to marry at the time.

We bought the most colorful Crocs we could find for ourselves, and for everyone in the wedding party, and then we got them matching clothes. I still remember my brother putting a black cummerbund around purple pants and asking if there was a particular reason we all looked like Teletubbies. And my friend who was in orange ended up looking like an escaped convict. Individually, we all looked kind of silly, but altogether it looked amazing!

Lots of other things made our wedding memorable. We made our own cake. We formed it into the shape of a sea turtle since that's one of our favorite animals. The food was a potluck, with local friends and family bringing favorite dishes of theirs that we requested. Far from feeling put upon, they loved that we remembered them cooking particular dishes.

Relatives gathered beautiful flowers from roadsides and arranged them on tables. Friends played live music for the ceremony.

For dancing at the reception, we used a playlist on an iPod, connected to a sound system that a friend of ours loaned us. The only downside to this setup was that as the evening wore on, some of my college friends got ahold of the iPod and skipped forward to some joke songs we never intended to play. On the bright side, I then got to see those same friends dance and sing along to "Ice, Ice Baby."

Some other things did not go exactly as planned. For instance, we ran out of forks. We didn't have a professional caterer, so we were borrowing all of the silverware from a local church, and one of my uncles left it all in the trunk of his car. My partner and I only discovered this when we went to serve ourselves and discovered there were no forks. Our guests, polite as ever, had made do with the silverware that the kitchen had. So I'm sure that some of them, like us, ended up eating ham loaf with a spoon.

All told, the entire wedding cost about $3,000. Half of that was for a professional photographer. We decided early on that we were not going to skimp on the photos. The rest covered our outdoor event fee, chair rentals, wine, champagne, the Crocs, and cake ingredients.

It was the best day of my life. At least, until our children were born. Our friends and family made our wedding incredible. As with most things, it's the people you're with, not the money you spend, that makes for the best memories.

20

STAY Together

"**I** 've got an idea for a new business," a friend tells you.

"Oh yeah? What are you thinking?" you ask.

"We take everything you own — all your cash, your home, stocks, bonds, retirement accounts, and all other assets — everything!" says your friend.

"Yeah, and then what?" you ask.

"Then we give away half of it!"

"Huh?"

"Oh, and here's the best part," your friend continues. "We also give away half of all the money you'll make in the future!"

Of course, no one would ever agree to this type of business proposition.

However, this is often what people end up with when they get divorced.

Okay, joking aside, let me state an unequivocal caveat here. If you are in a bad relationship that is abusive in *any* way, you should get out now. Your health (physical and mental) is worth more than any financial considerations. You should never stay in a toxic relationship for financial reasons. In fact, one of the best reasons for taking care of your finances is to ensure that you are never financially dependent on someone else.

But if you're just having the usual struggles that all couples face, then don't pinch pennies when it comes to trying to work it out. Pay whatever it takes to get good counseling — this will save you lots of money in the long run. I know several people who would have been able to retire years or even decades ago, but they're still working because they need to make payments to an ex-spouse. For these folks, divorce was the most costly financial decision they ever made.

So if you're looking to get your financial house in order, and your relationship is salvageable, then you should consider prioritizing anything you can do that will help you stay together.

For instance, if you're in a job that's causing lots of stress, and that stress is causing marital difficulties, it's worth thinking about looking for another job, even if it pays less. That loss of income pales in comparison to what you'll lose if your relationship falls apart.

And that's just from a financial standpoint. The research shows that there are many other long-term psychological, emotional, and health benefits from staying in a committed relationship.

21

Children Are CHEAP
(Not Really, But Hear Me Out)

N ote that if you do not have kids and never plan on having kids, you probably want to skip this chapter. I'll try to keep it brief and entertaining, but the information here really only applies to those of us who have kids.

Also, if you don't have kids, you might not want to read about pee, poop, and puke (and those topics are unavoidable when it comes to kids). That's likely not what you signed up for when you bought a book on personal finance. So I completely understand if you want to skip ahead.

Okay, for those of you still reading, let's dive into why children do not need to cost anywhere near the amount of money everyone says they do. My partner and I have three kids, and we've found lots of ways to get by without breaking the bank.

The notion that children are expensive comes from the fact that, if you want, you can easily spend every penny you have on your kids. Our consumer culture would love nothing more.

Need to walk your baby to the grocery store? Here, buy an electric stroller for $1,400 so you don't strain your arms pushing your baby down the street. (Yes, that product actually exists.)

When you need to feed your baby, why use regular utensils? Your baby is special, so you might as well splurge and get a literal silver spoon. The one that has diamonds embedded in it costs only $1,230! (Yes, this also exists.)

Or if you believe in contact parenting and want to put your newborn in a carrier, rather than using a stroller, why not get your baby carrier from Gucci? It's only $600!

Yes, all of these products — and many, many more — are available, and they will drain your bank account before your baby is old enough to say the word "Gucci." And, mind you, that's a baby word. ("Gucci, Gucci, goo!")

But you don't have to go bankrupt just because you decided to procreate. If your child is healthy, there are a lot of ways to lower — or entirely eliminate — some of the biggest expenses new parents face. It's not easy, but it's doable.

Minimize diapers

One significant baby expense is diapers. Until you have kids, you would not believe how many diapers they go through. When you're grocery shopping, you learn to buy more than one bag of diapers at a time. Otherwise, you're in a perpetual state of nonstop trips to the grocery store to refill the diaper supply that your baby already demolished while you were on your trip to the grocery store.

There are two ways to cut down on this major expense. The first is to use cloth diapers. They are way cheaper and way better for the environment. By some calculations, using cloth diapers saves a family around $1,000 per year per child.

Now I know that, despite the significant savings, cloth diapers are a hard sell. I heard an interview once where a mom explained that she was an environmentalist and wished she could switch to cloth diapers, but she just couldn't bring herself to do it. She said that before she would consider using cloth diapers, she would rather give up Styrofoam cups and have hot coffee poured directly into her bare hands.

So I understand if you want to stick with disposable diapers.

This brings me to the second way to cut down on these expenses: use fewer diapers. I know, I know: easy to say, impossible to do.

But there is a way. It requires learning about something called "elimination communication" and purchasing a baby potty. We got a potty from Baby Bjorn for around $10. You then hold your newborn on the potty as soon as you take off their diaper. It turns out that babies have a natural tendency to go to the bathroom when their bottoms are exposed to air. (If you've ever been peed on during a diaper change, you know exactly what I'm talking about.) By using that moment to have them pee in a potty, you can save hundreds of dollars in diapers.

Buy used clothes

In case you're new to parenting, let me tell you something about baby clothes. All of them — and I do mean every single item of baby clothing you own — will get puked, peed, and pooped on. Multiple times.

Keep that in mind if you're thinking about spending hundreds of dollars buying brand new clothes for your baby. Would you ever pay hundreds of dollars for anything else you knew would be soiled the day after you bought it?

Used baby clothes are easy to find. And they're usually in great shape: because babies grow so quickly, they don't have time to wear out their clothes. So save yourself some money and buy used baby clothes.

Live near the grandparents

Another great way to save money when you have kids is to live near your parents or your in-laws.

If you just spit out your drink, please accept my apologies. I know that some of you do not have good relationships with your parents. And I know that some of you have even worse relationships with your in-laws. If so, just skip this part of the book.

But if you have a good relationship with your parents or your in-laws, think about living near them when you have kids. Childcare is undoubtedly the biggest expense of having kids.

Yes, there are often subsidies available, and, yes, you can get a tax break for spending money on childcare. Make sure you look into both of these things! But the only free childcare I've ever seen is grandparents. I've heard that employers used to provide free childcare on-site, but I literally don't know a single person whose employer still does that.

If your parents or in-laws (or both!) are close enough to watch your kids, you'll save tens of thousands of dollars each year.

And, financial matters aside, I can say from personal experience that it's amazing to see your kids develop meaningful relationships with their grandparents.

Parenting is often the first time you realize just how much your own parents did to take care of you, and just how difficult that work was. This often leads people to reconnect with their parents in a more meaningful way. And there's no better way to strengthen those connections than to let them take care of your wonderful children. It's truly the best daycare imaginable, and it's free!

Avoid gadgets

News flash: your kid does not need a cell phone. Your kid certainly does not need a smartwatch either. Or any other myriad of gadgets that our consumer culture says everyone needs.

Choose your sports wisely

One final way you can save tens of thousands of dollars when raising kids is to make sure you choose your sports wisely. Want to be on the running team? Done! Ultimate frisbee? Soccer? Baseball? Yes, yes, and yes. These sports cost practically nothing.

How about cross-country skiing? That's a little pricier (you'll have some gear to buy), but you'll save thousands compared to downhill skiing.

When your kids ask you if they can play different sports, don't just say yes because they asked. Give some thought to how much it will cost if they decide to keep playing that sport for the rest of their life.

Get the tax breaks

Don't have kids just to save money on your taxes. But if you do have kids, you will want to hug them every time you fill out your taxes. When you do your taxes online, you get to click the up-arrow next to the line asking about dependents. With each click, you quickly see the red "amount owed" number go down, and then, if you have three kids like me, you usually see it turn green, signifying a refund.

But don't make the mistake I made of mentioning to your kids that you're getting a tax refund because of them. My kids, being quite clever, immediately started asking whether they would get this money, and I found myself at a bit of a loss trying to explain why they didn't.

22

Three Types of DEBT: the Good, the Bad, and the Ugly

There are three types of debt: the good, the bad, and the ugly. Let's tackle them in reverse order.

The Ugly

When I was out walking my dog the other day, I came across a piece of paper on the side of the road. I picked it up to bring it home to recycle. When I looked at it, I noticed that it was a bill from a hardware store.

The bill showed a previous balance of $2,305 and a recent payment of $39. But the new balance was a whopping $3,102! This was due to $836 in "deferred interest."

In my opinion, this should be criminal. This particular store credit card claimed to have a 26% annual interest rate. That is bad enough as it is. But what actually happened is that the card let the person pay 0% interest for several months, and then they got hit with, in effect, a 435% interest rate!

No, I'm not missing a decimal point there. A one-month charge of $836 on a $2,305 bill works out to an annual interest rate of 435%.

This is what I call "ugly" debt. And I'd say the same even if this hardware store had not used a sleazy trick like "deferred interest."

All credit card debt, including store credit cards, is ugly debt. Same for payday loans. Ugly debt. The interest on those is outlandish, arguably criminal.

In my mind, the ugly debt category covers everything that charges 8% or more in interest.

And when it comes to ugly debt, I'm also going to add in loans from friends and family. Those may not have the 20% interest rates that credit cards often have, but they come at a cost that weighs heavily on your conscience.

Avoid ugly debt. Period. Pay off every credit card in full every month. Never take a payday loan. Never borrow from friends and family.

"But what about ...?" Let me stop you right there. Never means never.

If you have ugly debt, your top financial priority should always be to get rid of it. Later in this chapter, I'll talk in detail about how to tackle debt so you get rid of it forever.

The Bad

Now if you remember back to my story from an early chapter about how I nearly paid $1,000 for an audiobook, you're probably thinking to yourself, "What a hypocrite!"

It's true. When I was in law school, I built up around $10,000 in credit card debt. That's why I would have lost around $1,000 if the interest rate on that particular card had increased when I tried to buy an audiobook.

In my defense, that $10,000 in debt was not ugly debt. It was merely bad debt. That particular credit card charged only 4.9% in interest. That was a significantly lower interest rate than the student loans I was taking out at the time.

But it still wasn't a good choice. Even debt at 4.9% is bad debt. Particularly because that credit card debt was for consumer goods, which always depreciate in value. (We'll talk about appreciating assets like homes in a minute when we cover the topic of good debt.)

The bad debt category covers things like car loans, student loans, and home equity lines of credit (HELOCs). These are consumer purchases with interest rates that can be as low as 3% or as high as 8%. (If you ever get a car loan that is less than 3%, it's not because you got a great deal. It means you paid more for the car than you should have, so they gave you a break on financing.)

This debt is all bad debt because it's a drain on your finances. Now I'm not saying that you should have never taken out the debt in the first place. You may have needed a car. You may have needed to get student loans for undergraduate or graduate school. And you may have needed to take out a HELOC to pay for necessary repairs to your home.

And these are all expenses that likely continue to benefit you every day. If you have a car loan, you're benefiting from having the car. It gets you to work and back. It likely has many safety features that older cars don't have.

If you have student loans, you're probably making much more money at your job than you would make without the education you received. Not always. (Many people take out student loans but then never finish school, or end up working in an entirely different field.) But chances are that you made the right choice taking out these student loans.

My point here is not that you should avoid bad debt. But once you have it, you should try to get rid of it.

Getting rid of bad debt is important, but because the interest rate is 8% or lower, getting rid of it does not need to be your top priority. That's what makes bad debt different from ugly debt. So, for instance, if you have an auto loan at

3%, you're probably better off paying only the minimum on that loan and directing additional funds to your investment accounts.

That said, even for loans that have interest rates as low as 3%, that's still money that you're effectively flushing down the toilet every month. These loans are doing you no good at all, and they could be holding you back from really ramping up your investment contributions. The sooner you can get rid of bad debt, the better.

When it comes to debt, always remember: interest is never in your interest.

The Good

Is there any kind of debt that is good? Kind of.

Many financial advisors talk about "good debt," though they define that term differently. In my view, the only way something could be considered good debt is if it meets both of the following criteria: (1) it has a very low interest rate (certainly less than 8% and probably closer to 3%), and (2) it is for an asset that appreciates in value (like a home or other real estate).

So, for instance, if you bought a new home in 2020, you probably took on good debt. This is because you likely got a great mortgage rate like 3%. And if you chose your home wisely, then the value of your home should go up by at least 3% every year. As a result, you make more in appreciation than you pay in interest every year. This means your financial net worth increases from owning this asset.

Note that real estate is about the only type of good debt out there. The only other good debt worth mentioning is starting a business. Taking out a loan to start a business can be considered good debt, but it should only be done with great caution. Just 30% of small businesses last 10 years, but nearly every one of those business owners is certain that their business is going to be one of the ones that makes it.

Don't get me wrong: I have nothing against starting a business. It can be an amazing way to improve your finances. I do, however, recommend finding a way to do it without going into debt. A good book on how to do this is *The $100 Startup*, by Chris Guillebeau.

What about cars? Sorry, but cars are never good debt. They depreciate at an astounding rate the moment you drive them off the lot. Even when you buy used (as you should), the value keeps going down each year you have it.

What about art, sports cards, fine wines, and comic books? Sounds like an amazing birthday party! But you shouldn't ever go into debt to buy these things.

That's why I think real estate is usually the only type of good debt worth incurring. And even with real estate, you need to know what you're doing before you take on debt. Lots of people thought they were taking on "good debt" when they bought new homes in the years leading up to 2008. They later discovered that home values do not always go up. So make sure you're careful even when taking on good debt.

How to tackle debt

The best method for eliminating debt is to start with whatever debt has the highest interest rate, and put every spare dollar you have into paying off those loans. You of course have to make the minimum payments on all your other debts, but any extra money you have should go toward the debt with the highest interest rate. Once that debt is paid off, you proceed to tackling the next highest interest rate. As each debt is paid off, you have more money to put toward the next one.

Paying off the loan with the highest interest rate is known as the "avalanche" method of debt reduction. I call it the math way. Because that's all it is. If you have one debt that charges you 10% in interest, and one that charges 20%, then you should always pay off the 20% debt first.

You're probably thinking, "Well, duh, of course, that's how you do it." If that's you, then feel free to go ahead and skip the next paragraph.

The other way to reduce debt is known as the "snowball" method. The snowball method is when you focus on paying off the debt with the lowest amount due, to try to gather small wins that encourage you to keep going. So if you owe $1,000 at 10% interest, and $2,000 at 20% interest, then you'd direct any additional funds toward paying off the $1,000 debt, even though it's at a lower interest rate. You would continue doing this until someone hit you in the face with a snowball. At that point, you'd realize that you were paying more money than you should, and you'd start using the avalanche method. I'm kidding, of course. The snowball method has its place. Many people get overwhelmed with trying to pay off large debts. If paying off small debts will keep you motivated, then go for it. Any method of paying off debt is better than no method at all.

Also, you can always switch your method of debt repayment. For instance, when you're just beginning to tackle your debt, you may want to start with the snowball method to gather small wins. Later on, you can switch to the avalanche method to minimize your interest payments.

What about refinancing?

When it comes to debt, you also always want to look into refinancing. In other parts of this book, I talk in more detail about refinancing homes and student loans. But refinancing can save you money on consumer debt as well.

For instance, if you have a car loan that's charging you over 5%, you may be able to find a much lower loan, particularly if you have good credit. As I mentioned earlier in this book, most people don't know that you can refinance a car you already own, so long as you have equity in it. If there are no refinancing fees, you could save lots of money by switching lenders.

Also, don't be afraid of negotiating with lenders. As discussed in an earlier chapter ("Always ASK for Discounts"), debt from credit cards can be negotiated. You may be able to work out a deal with your credit card company to repay only a portion of what you owe. As a reminder, when you negotiate over a debt you already owe, you run the risk of hurting your credit score. So make sure you know all the consequences if you take this route.

23

INSURE Don't Waste

"**J**ust two minor accidents," my dad calmly announced as he and my brother walked into the house. We were all wondering what the yelling had been about.

"I can't believe it," my brother said. "Dad managed to back into not one, but *two* cars in our driveway!"

Insurance serves an important purpose. If you're my dad, you need lots of it. For the rest of us, you want to take a more measured approach.

Insurance is always a tricky balancing act. It is money that usually (hopefully, in fact!) never gets you anything. You read that right. The best-case scenario is that you never get a penny back from your insurance policies. After all, that means you've avoided accidents.

This does not mean that your insurance payments were a waste of money. I remember a friend of mine who got into rock climbing. He told me that he frequently makes it to the top of a climb without falling, and he thinks "I could have done that without the rope." True, but that doesn't mean he wasted time setting up the rope. At some point, on some climb, he will fall.

You need a rope. If you wouldn't go rock climbing without a rope, then you understand why you need insurance.

But how much? The best advice is to get the minimum amount of insurance needed to cover catastrophic events.

Remember, this is not one-size-fits-all. If you're my dad, you need much more coverage. But most of us can get away with a lesser amount.

Do not overinsure. The reason you don't want to overinsure is that it's expensive. And you could be using that money for better things. A caveat here is that if your employer subsidizes your insurance (for instance, by covering 80% of health care premiums), then you may want to get more coverage than you normally would. But if you're paying full freight, then you don't want to buy more than you need. Below I'll get into the details of how to save money on your insurance.

First of all, let's talk about what insurance you need. Most people should always have at least these five types of insurance: health, homeowners (if you own a home), car, disability, and life.

Health insurance

If you have an employer, they probably provide you with heavily subsidized health insurance. Take some time to read through any options you have and make sure you select the plan that works best for you and your family.

If you're self-employed, or already retired, you've got some work to do to find the best health insurance option. Do your research and make sure you look at every available option.

There's no faster train to the poor house than an unforeseen and uninsured health incident. No matter how healthy you are now, that can change at a moment's notice.

According to a 2019 article in the American Journal of Public Health (*Medical Bankruptcy: Still Common Despite the Affordable Care Act*), around two out of three bankruptcies are the direct or indirect result of a medical issue. Don't let this be you. As hard as it is to pay hundreds, or even thousands, of dollars every month for health insurance, it's worth it.

Again, you don't need to overinsure. If you're young and healthy, then your best option may be to get a high-deductible plan. High-deductible plans are especially attractive because they allow you to participate in a Health Savings Account. (See more about the tax benefits of Health Savings Accounts in the upcoming chapter on "TAXES Are Not Inevitable.")

On the other hand, if you expect to have health issues, or you just don't want to risk it, you may want to spend more to get a more comprehensive healthcare plan.

Finally, if you live in the United States and ever find yourself in need of major surgery or significant dental work, make sure to look into medical tourism. You may be able to fly to another country and receive equally good or better medical or dental care for less than what you'd pay to get the same procedure done at home.

Homeowners' insurance

If you're going to own a home, then you have to insure it. Get a good policy that will cover the cost of a full rebuild if anything happens to your home. If you're in a flood-prone area, make sure you have flood insurance as well.

To save money on your homeowners' insurance, you'll want to shop around. Every year. To save even more, you'll probably want to go with a high deductible (like $1,000 or even $2,500). It's incredibly unlikely you'll ever make a claim, so you're usually better off going with a high deductible to minimize your monthly payments.

Car insurance

The last time our car insurance was up for renewal, I asked how much we could save if we increased the deductible on both of our cars from $250 to $500. The answer was $160! Every year!

This was a no-brainer. We would have to have *two accidents* every three years to make it worth it to pay the extra $160 in premiums for the lower-deductible plan. Even then we'd only save $20 because the $500 saved through lower-deductible payments would be mostly offset by $480 extra in premium payments over these three years.

And to save this $20, we'd have to not just have two accidents, but two accidents that were worth reporting to insurance. In general, whenever you report an accident, your insurance premiums go up. Often for many years. So if you back into a tree and do $500 worth of damage to your car, you're better off paying for that out-of-pocket even if you have a $250 deductible. The $250 you'd get from the insurance company would be more than offset by the higher premiums you'd pay over the next few years.

So, since it's only worth it to report larger accidents (generally those that cost $1,000 or more), you effectively already have a high deductible. If you're my dad, you can count on having several of those major accidents every year, so it's worth it to keep a low $250 deductible and save $250 every time you have one of those accidents. But for the rest of us, as soon as you have $500 or more in your savings account, a higher deductible is usually the way to go.

Disability insurance

As Ric Edelman notes in *The Truth About Money*, your biggest financial asset is your ability to produce an income. Disability insurance provides you and your family with a percentage of your income (usually around 60%) if you are injured and cannot work.

Many employers offer free or heavily discounted disability insurance. Make sure you're enrolled in whatever plan your employer offers.

Social security provides disability insurance as well, but it's renowned for being incredibly difficult to get. Around 60% of all applications for social security disability benefits are denied.

You should also look into getting private disability insurance, even if you're already covered by a workplace plan. A surprisingly high percentage of employees become disabled at some point in their careers. You want to make sure you're covered if this happens to you.

When searching for a disability insurance policy, make sure you know what to look for. In particular, you should avoid "any-occupation" policies. Those policies provide benefits only if your disability is so severe that you cannot do *any* job. The far better policy is known as "own-occupation." This policy provides benefits when your disability prevents you from doing the work you're currently doing.

Life insurance

If anyone else depends on your income, then you also need life insurance.

There are two kinds of life insurance: term and whole life.

Term insurance is far cheaper than whole life insurance. It covers you for a specific term (like 15, 20, or 25 years). You pay premiums each month you have it and can cancel it at any time. If you die while your policy is active, your family gets paid the full amount you signed up for. If you survive, you do not get any of your money back.

Whole life insurance is permanent insurance and works more like an investment account. Your monthly premiums are far higher than term insurance, but you're entitled to get back a portion of the amount you pay, even if you later cancel your policy.

Whole life insurance may be worth it if you fall into one of the following three categories: (1) you are a multi-millionaire and are looking for advanced ways to minimize taxes, (2) you have a family history of early death that makes you unlikely to qualify for term insurance, or (3) you like donating your hard-earned money to life insurance agents.

For the rest of us, term insurance is far better.

Term insurance is incredibly cheap these days. When I turned 40 in 2020, and the coronavirus was in full swing, I decided it was time to get life insurance. I found a website that compares different policy options. I ended up getting a 15-year $500,000 policy for just $20 per month.

One quick tip: when you apply for life insurance (or any insurance for that matter), make sure you answer every question fully and honestly. You do not want to give the insurer an excuse to issue a denial should you or your family ever need to make a claim.

What about long-term care insurance and umbrella insurance?

Let me mention two more forms of insurance that you may want to consider purchasing.

One is long-term care insurance. Unfortunately, Medicare generally does not cover long-term care services. This means that if you or a loved one ends up in a nursing home, you could be facing hundreds of thousands of dollars in unforeseen expenses. This is why many people choose to buy long-term care insurance.

That said, the problem with long-term care insurance is that it is incredibly expensive. This is why you should also think about other options. You may be better off building up a larger balance in your investment portfolio or making sure you have enough equity in your home to pay for long-term care if you need it.

The other insurance policy to consider is an umbrella policy. An umbrella insurance policy covers you if you get sued and ordered to pay more money than your auto and homeowners' insurance policies cover. This is worth considering if you have a high financial net worth. If you have a high financial net worth, then you are at risk of losing hundreds of thousands of dollars (or even millions) if you get sued. An umbrella policy can fill this gap.

What's great about umbrella policies is that they're cheap. For instance, a $1 million umbrella policy might cost as little as $150 per year. This is usually worth it to prevent potentially devastating losses.

How to save money on all of your insurance policies

The three best ways to save money on insurance are the following: (1) shop around, (2) generally look for the highest deductible you can afford, and (3) renegotiate every year.

One more thing on insurance: do not ever buy extended warranties. If the extended warranty were a good deal (mathematically speaking), then the seller would never offer it.

Here's a case-in-point: my dad once bought a "bumper-to-bumper" warranty on a car. When the car radio broke, I brought it to the dealer to get it fixed. I mentioned to the man at the front desk that the car was under warranty.

"That doesn't cover the radio," he said.

"What do you mean?" I asked.

"The radio isn't covered by the warranty," he said.

"We got an extended warranty," I said. "It's the full bumper-to-bumper one."

"I know," he said. "That doesn't cover the radio."

"Last I checked," I replied, "the radio was located between the two bumpers."

Despite my infallible logic, we were out of luck. Like I said, extended warranties are written for the seller, not the customer. Save your money and don't buy them.

24

AVOID CONTINGENT-FEE AND PERCENTAGE-BASED FINANCIAL ADVISORS

Let's say you need a new primary care doctor. You've narrowed it down to two. You then find out that one doctor receives kickbacks from pharmaceutical companies every time she prescribes a medication. The other doctor does not. Which one do you choose?

The same goes for financial advisors, financial planners, brokers, and all the other names used by anyone who gets paid to give advice on how to invest. Do not *ever* choose one that receives a kickback for getting you to invest. Sadly — and inexplicably — the financial profession allows advisors to receive kickbacks. A kickback can come in many forms. Here are a few of them:

- **Commissions.** Why invest 100% of your money, when you can give some of that hard-earned cash to your financial advisor every time they buy a fund for you?

- **Assets Under Management.** Do you like paying taxes? If so, assets under management fees are for you! Like commissions, they skim a percentage off the top. Usually only around 1%, but it's charged every ... single ... year. Over your lifetime, this adds up to tens or even hundreds of thousands of dollars.

- **Front-End Loads.** If you have $100,000 to invest, then instead of spending five minutes purchasing the fund you want for free online, you can ask your financial advisor to do it for a mere $5,000! Great deal, huh?

- **Back-End Loads.** Love this one. Why get charged only when you buy when you can also get charged when you sell?

- **Performance-Based Fees.** On the off-chance your broker outperforms the market, you get to pay them extra. Of course, when they underperform the market — which they usually do — they don't pay you anything.

- **Retainers.** Since you're already paying your advisor tons of money whenever they do anything for you, why not also pay them when they don't do anything at all? Like assets under management fees, retainers are thousands of dollars in annual costs just for the privilege of having a financial advisor.

- **Robo-Advisor Fees.** True, these are usually far lower than what you'll pay for human advisors — for instance, 0.25% of assets under management, rather than 1% — but these fees add up as well. And they're entirely unnecessary.

While most things in the world of personal finance are nuanced and subject to multiple interpretations, some things are black and white. This is one of them. Do not — ever, under any circumstances — pay any of the above fees.

These fees are ongoing charges (similar to monthly charges). You should never pay commissions, fees for assets under management, loads, or any of the other fees listed above. If that is the only lesson you take from this book, I'll have saved you thousands, tens of thousands, or even hundreds of thousands of dollars. You're welcome.

There are only two fees you should ever pay when it comes to your investments: (1) expense ratios, which should never be more than 0.25%, and (2) an hourly or annual fee to a *fee-only* financial advisor.

The phrase "fee-only" is key. If the financial advisor is commission-based, do not use them. And if they're "fee-*based*," avoid that as well! A "fee-based" advisor can charge commissions, in addition to fees. A "fee-*only*" financial advisor can never receive a commission for a product they sell you. No kickbacks are allowed.

Is it enough to be "fee-only"? No! If you decide to hire a financial advisor, you also need to make sure that they only charge an hourly or annual rate, or perhaps a flat fixed fee for a financial plan.

Many fee-only financial advisors charge a percentage of assets under management. Robo-advisors, brokerage firms (like Vanguard and Fidelity), and other companies (like Personal Capital) do the same for their financial services. These fees generally range from around 0.25% for robo-advisors to around 1% for personalized advice. Again, this does not sound like much, but it adds up quickly!

And these fees are completely unnecessary. Consider this: let's say you want to buy a new home. One realtor tells you they charge a 6% sales commission when you buy. (This is typical.) But another realtor offers to charge only 1%. The catch is that you have to pay that 1% on the entire value of the home *every year*.

So if you're buying a $200,000 home, you would write a check to the first realtor for $12,000. If you went with the second realtor, you'd write a check for at least $2,000 every single year. In fact, because home values (like your portfolio) usually increase in value every year, these annual checks would quickly increase. For instance, if your home value went up just 3% each year, then by the end of your 30-year mortgage, you'd be paying around $5,000 every year. And why exactly are you sending a realtor a check for $5,000 every year? Because 30 years earlier they spent one hour helping you choose a home. You would never agree to pay that. Yet, that's basically what you're doing when you agree to pay a percentage of assets under management.

Also, if you're going with a financial advisor, make sure that, in addition to being fee-only, they're a fiduciary. That means they're legally and ethically bound to put your interests first.

I can't believe I even have to say this, but, inexplicably, many financial advisors are allowed to offer you advice that is not in your best interests, so long as it's considered "suitable." This makes my head hurt.

Quite frankly, if there were any logic to the financial world, every financial advisor would be required to be a fiduciary. In my opinion, the only advice that is "suitable" is advice that is solely in the best interests of the investor, free from any conflicts or even potential conflicts of interest.

As Peter Mallouk explains in his recent book *The Path*, the fact that a fiduciary duty is not a mandated federal requirement of all financial advisors speaks to the lobbying power of the financial industry. This is why he concludes that "the financial services industry is broken," and that "if you have a typical advisor, the odds are that you would be better off without one."

Hopefully, by now, you have a healthy skepticism of financial advisors. That's good. The reality is that most of us do not need a financial advisor at all.

Not surprisingly, financial advisors rarely admit that they are not needed. Many won't admit this even if they subscribe to the simple investment principles described later in this book (using a small group of low-fee index funds and periodically rebalancing). They know that, with the internet, everyone can easily choose an asset allocation and open their own accounts directly with Vanguard, Fidelity, or Schwab. No financial advisor needed.

Yet they insist that everyone still needs a financial advisor. Why? It's simple: they want to believe their jobs are more important than they are. Sorry to be blunt, but this is the only explanation.

In several articles and books that I've read, financial advisors present themselves as though they are as necessary as doctors. You wouldn't ever treat a serious illness on your own, would you? Then why do you think you can handle your investments on your own?

Hogwash. Investing is not brain surgery.

A better analogy would be picking out Band-Aids at a pharmacy: "Hi, Doctor Williamson, it's Kyle. I'm standing in aisle three of Walgreens and looking at the waterproof ones and a kind that claims to have some sort of antibacterial agent in it. Now the flexible ones look good for the paper cut I have, but I'm also thinking that the antibacterial agent would help avoid infection. Would you mind coming down here and helping me choose?"

You would never use your doctor that way. And you shouldn't use financial advisors that way either.

So who does need to hire a fee-only financial advisor? I would say that there are three groups of people who definitely should do so.

First, if you know you don't have the discipline to handle your investments yourself. For instance, you may know yourself well enough to know that you'd sell your stocks if the market tanked, rather than buying more stocks when they're on sale. As wise folks from Socrates to Shakespeare have said, know yourself. If you need someone's help, then by all means get it.

Second, if you have a complex tax situation (for instance, because you're inheriting a large amount of money), then you need professional advice. You do not want to try to navigate complex tax laws on your own and then find out you've lost thousands of dollars to Uncle Sam because you did it wrong.

Third, if you have a significant amount of assets (for instance, a million dollars or more), then you should probably be working with a fee-only financial advisor. Don't be scared off by what I've written above. Just do your research and find a fee-only advisor who is also a fiduciary.

Part IV
INVEST WISELY

25

INVEST THE SMART AND GREEN WAY

I f you have implemented any of the tips from previous chapters, you should already be making more and spending less. This means more money in your bank account. In these next few chapters, we'll talk about ways to invest that money wisely.

Before we jump into the next few chapters on investing, let me reiterate the disclaimer I gave at the beginning of this book about how I am *not* providing investment advice. Like the rest of this book, these chapters are purely informational. If you want advice on investing, you'll need to hire a professional financial advisor — see the previous chapter about what to look for in choosing one.

Let me also reiterate that when it comes to investments, past performance is not an assurance of future returns. That's not just a disclaimer: it's the truth. Anyone who tells you otherwise is lying. Investing is always a guessing game and it always involves risk. Nothing is guaranteed.

There is only one sure-fire way to make money in the stock market: insider trading. Insider trading works because secret knowledge about a company is the only way to know for certain that a stock price will soar or crater. The only problem is it's illegal. Just ask Martha Stewart.

Please do NOT ever, ever, ever engage in insider trading. Going to jail does not aid your journey toward financial independence (although I suppose you could categorize it as retiring early). If you picked up this book because you were looking for a way to get rich quick, even through illegal means, you picked up the wrong book. That book is much shorter and goes something like this:

YOUR 3-STEP GUIDE TO FINANCIAL FREEDOM

(1) Get $1 million by robbing a bank.
(2) Use insider trading to convert it to $2 million.
(3) Buy and hold three low-fee index funds: domestic stocks, international stocks, and bonds.

Pretty simple, huh?

But assuming you do not want to go to jail, let's talk about how you can make money in the stock market. I'll give you a hint: forget Steps 1 and 2 above, but do pay attention to Step 3.

That's it.

If you want, you can read a bunch of books about this (like I did), but you'll almost certainly reach the same conclusion I have: buy and hold low-fee index funds. John C. Bogle, the founder of Vanguard, figured this out a long time ago. One of his best books, *The Little Book of Common Sense Investing*, explains in detail why buying low-fee index funds, and holding on to them for at least 10 years, is the best way to invest. I also recommend reading *The Simple Path to Wealth* by J.L. Collins and *How to Invest for Retirement*, by Anthony S. Park. If you want something shorter and more succinct, it takes less than an hour to read *If You Can: How Millennials Can Get Rich Slowly*, by William J. Bernstein.

Okay, there's a little bit more to investing than just knowing about low-fee index funds. There are four things to focus on when putting together your investment plan: (1) choice of investments (which stock and bond funds to buy), (2) asset allocation and rebalancing (how much of your portfolio is in stocks and bonds), (3) contributions (how much you're investing and when), and (4) taxes (how to structure your investments to minimize taxes).

In the next few chapters, we'll address each of these concepts.

Throughout these chapters, I'll also talk about the overlap between smart investing and green investing. As I'll explain in more detail below, I think it's important to consider green values when deciding how to invest your money. Not only is this the right thing to do, but it can also make you more money.

26

How to CHOOSE Investments

Before you can invest, you need to know where to put your money.
The best financial advisors will tell you that you should not invest in individual stocks. The price of every stock is the result of a collective group of people looking at every facet of a company to determine what it is worth. And many of those people have way more knowledge than you or I will ever have about a particular company.

Simply put, choosing to buy stock in a single company is speculation. You might get lucky. Much more likely you'll get burned. And it's guaranteed you'll waste time and lose sleep trying to figure out whether your company is going to do well or go bankrupt.

Those who have studied stock markets have almost universally concluded that there's a much better way to invest: buy and hold the whole stock market through low-fee index funds. The historical average return of the stock market, over the long run, is around 10%!

You cannot count on those returns in the future (remember that past performance does not guarantee future results), and inflation will likely eat away 2-3% of your annual gains. But if you buy and hold low-fee index funds over the long term (at least 10 years), you give yourself a much better chance of making money than if you were to choose individual stocks.

And you can do the same for international stock and bond funds. They can be purchased through low-fee index funds as well.

What does "buy and hold" mean?

Buy and hold means committing to keeping your stocks and bonds for the long run. And it means real commitment. There is no such thing as a partial buy-and-hold strategy.

So, for instance, you can't buy and hold only when the stock market is doing well. The whole point of the buy-and-hold strategy is to keep your investments even when the stock market plummets.

This is much harder than it sounds, so your commitment to a buy-and-hold strategy must be rock solid. Even when you think you have a better strategy, you have to hold firm. Otherwise, it will not work.

While most of my stories about my dad involve him making poor financial decisions, one place my dad shines is when it comes to commitment and resolve. He has always been good at being decisive. He knows that you're usually better off making a decision and sticking to it, even if it's not perfect. You need that type of resolve when it comes to investing.

The best illustration of my dad's resolve comes from when I was six years old and my family traveled to Montreal.

One afternoon we were riding the subway and my parents couldn't figure out which stop to take. When we pulled into a station, they were still debating whether it was our stop.

My dad said yes, this was our stop. Then my mom said no, it's definitely the next stop.

The only problem was that as soon as I heard my dad say that this was our stop and before my mom corrected him, I stepped off the subway. Then the doors closed.

I turned around and saw my parents on the other side of the thick glass subway doors.

My dad looked straight at me and put on the most serious and stern face I've ever seen (then or any time since). Although I could not hear what he was saying through the thick glass door, his lips clearly formed the words "STAY THERE!"

He used his index finger to emphasize each of those words, pointing directly at me while he said "STAY!" and then again while he said "THERE!"

A second later, the subway train was gone. I looked around and saw that I was all alone, except for a homeless man sitting on a piece of cardboard. He seemed preoccupied and didn't appear to notice that he was now sharing the subway station with a six-year-old.

I wasn't scared. In fact, I was a bit annoyed at my dad's instructions. I had heard my mom state clearly that the next station was the right one, so I didn't see why they should now circle back to get me. It seemed to make much more sense for my family to wait for me at the next stop while I grabbed the next train. But my dad's instructions were crystal clear, so I stayed where I was.

Half an hour later, my dad arrived. We hopped on the next train together and met up with the rest of my family at the next station.

So what does all of this have to do with buying and holding low-fee index funds? I think of the buy-and-hold strategy as my dad standing inside the subway train and telling me to "STAY THERE!" It's one of the few clear, hard-and-fast rules in personal finance, and it's one that you really have to follow even when you think it doesn't make sense.

There is an enormous amount of research about how the average investor receives much lower returns than the overall stock market. The main reason for this is that the average investor often gets scared when the market drops and cashes out their investments at the worst possible time.

When you pull out of the stock market during a dip, you lock in your losses. This guarantees you lose money because you're selling your stocks at a time when prices are low. More experienced investors know that after stock prices fall, they're on sale, and that's a time to buy, not sell. Or as Warren Buffet says, "Be greedy when others are fearful, and fearful when others are greedy."

The worst thing you can do for your portfolio is to sell stocks during a market dip. You need to be in it for the long run. When the market goes down, ignore those who say to cash out or to convert all your stocks into bonds. Picture my dad pointing his finger and saying, "STAY THERE!"

What's so great about low-fee index funds?

As the books mentioned in the previous chapter explain in detail, low-fee index funds are passively managed and have big advantages over actively managed stocks and mutual funds. Here are a few:

- **Diversification.** Index funds invest in an entire sector of the stock market. In fact, the most touted low-fee index fund is Vanguard's Total Stock Market Index Fund (VTSAX), which literally covers the entire stock market. Fidelity's Total Market Index Fund (FSKAX) does the same. This gives you maximum diversification, particularly if you invest in at least the following three low-fee index funds: a domestic stock index fund like VTSAX or FSKAX, an international stock index fund, and a bond index fund.

- **Lower fees and taxes.** Because index funds are passively managed, they charge much lower fees than actively managed funds. For instance, VTSAX has an expense ratio of 0.04%, and FSKAX is even less. By comparison, the expense ratio of many actively managed mutual funds is between 0.5% and 1%.

  Also, index funds generally incur much lower transaction fees because passively managed funds have a lower turnover ratio (fewer trades) than actively managed funds. This also means that index funds are usually more tax-efficient than actively managed mutual funds.

  Those savings in annual expense ratios, transaction costs, and taxes can add up to as much as 3% per year. And I haven't even mentioned the fact that actively managed funds may also charge a sales commission (known as a "load").

  While a percent (or two or three) here or there might not sound like much (after all, 1% is only $10 per $1,000 invested), it makes an enormous difference in the long run. If your investments generate a 10% return ($100 per $1,000 invested), then paying a 1% fee every year means you're losing 10% of your total returns! Add in the impact of compounding, and those fees add up quickly.

- **Greater historical returns.** Over the long run, total stock market index funds have performed better than nearly every actively managed mutual fund. This is a shocking fact, and most people have trouble believing it. But it's true. There has been an enormous amount of research comparing actively managed funds to index funds, and index funds win out nearly every time, particularly once fees are taken into account. As Karen Langley noted in a March 11, 2021 *Wall Street Journal* article titled *Stock Pickers Trailed Market Again in Roller Coaster 2020*, the year 2020 marked the eleventh consecutive year in which the majority of actively managed funds performed worse than the S&P 500 index fund.

  One reason index funds usually perform so well is that they have a self-cleaning function. You know, like your oven! Although I have no idea how self-cleaning works on an oven, I can explain how it works with index funds. What happens is that the worst-performing funds can only go down so much before they drop out of the index. The best performing funds, on the other hand, can continue to go up — there is no cap on their growth. This limits your losses, while your gains are unlimited.

  But what about those five-star funds that outperformed the market last year? Surely that's a better investment, right? No, it's not. In fact, buying last year's highest-ranking fund is almost certain to lose you money, compared to buying a low-fee index fund. This is because any fund that did great last year is probably going to have inflated prices. This means you're buying high, and thus more likely to have to sell low — the exact opposite of what you want to do when you're investing.

  What about Warren Buffett? Doesn't he pick specific funds and usually outperform the market? Yes, he does, but he's a unicorn. So is Peter Lynch. For every one of them, there are hundreds of active fund managers who will charge you higher fees for the privilege of making you less money. As J.L. Collins has noted, when you look at an investment term of 30 years or more, *less than 1%* of active fund managers have outperformed passive funds.

- **Less time consuming.** You have better things to do with your time than research stocks and mutual funds. Yes, please finish reading this chapter, and do some more reading to learn the basics of investing. But do not waste your time trying to beat the market.

  It's a loser's game, on two fronts. First, you'll likely lose out financially. This is because no matter how much research you do, you're unlikely to ever beat the market.

  Second, you're guaranteed to lose hours, days, weeks, months, and maybe even years of your life trying to outsmart other investors. Try calculating the hourly rate on that, and my guess is that even if you succeed, you'll have earned less than minimum wage.

  Again, I'll pass. I've got better things to do with my time.

For these reasons, the FIRE community generally subscribes to the advice that your best bet for investing is to place your money in low-fee index funds. I agree.

Consider green investing

But I also think it's important to consider green values when deciding how to invest your money. I say this for two reasons. First, it's the right thing to do. Second, it can make you more money.

Your personal budget (how you spend your money) is a value statement. Consider the following thought experiment. Let's say you're hungry and you see two identical-looking restaurants. The menus are the same, the decor looks the same, and the prices are the same. The only difference is that one has a sign saying, "All profits donated to charity," while the other restaurant has a sign that says, "Help us make more money to buy cigarettes for young children." Which restaurant would you pick? Whenever possible, I try to avoid giving my money to evildoers.

Thankfully, it's easier than ever to have our cake and eat it too. At least two major investment groups, Vanguard and Fidelity, now offer low-fee index funds that are also socially responsible. Fidelity now offers socially responsible versions of all three of the low-fee index funds that most investors seek: a domestic stock index fund (Fidelity US Sustainability Index Fund or FITLX), an international stock index fund (Fidelity International Sustainability Index Fund or FNIDX), and a bond index fund (Fidelity Sustainability Bond Index Fund or FNDSX).

These mutual funds have all the benefits of other index funds (including diversification and low fees) and are also socially and environmentally responsible. Granted, when you go with socially responsible funds, you will not be as diversified as a total stock market index. You've intentionally screened out companies that do not meet certain criteria. Also, the fees are higher than what you would pay for regular low-fee index funds. For instance, Vanguard's FTSE Social Index Fund Admiral Shares (VFTAX) has an expense ratio of 0.14, rather than the 0.04 that you can get for VTSAX. However, even 0.14 is still way below what most mutual funds charge.

There's a strong case to be made that socially responsible investing is just as profitable as conventional investing and may even give you an edge. The research is bearing this out. For instance, Saiful Arefeen and Koji Shimada have published a study called *Performance and Resilience of Socially Responsible Investing (SRI) and Conventional Funds during Different Shocks in 2016: Evidence from Japan* (January 10, 2020) (available at mdpi.com). That study concluded that socially responsible investing is comparable to conventional investing and can provide a competitive edge, particularly during turbulent times.

It makes sense that any company that abides by socially responsible criteria, including environmental awareness and sound environmental practices, is more likely to do well in the long term. These companies are thinking about the long-term impact of their operations. Consumer demand for these socially and environmentally responsible goods continues to increase, and it is difficult to see that ever changing.

If it seems too good to be true …

Whether you go with regular low-fee index funds or socially responsible index funds, let me add one more word of caution: if you dive into the world of investing, you'll discover lots of financial advisors who think they have a better strategy than low-fee index funds. Don't believe them.

For instance, I stumbled across a book about how to make a "safe" 8% return on bonds. The book mocked those who rely on index funds for their retirement. It made particular fun of those who rely on the 4% Rule and take "only" 4% of their nest egg every year. The book's premise was that it was, of course, far better to make 8% on safe bond investments, and then you can withdraw *twice* as much every year without ever touching the principal! Sounds pretty great, huh? And a lot of what was in there made sense — after all, it was investing in bonds, which most people consider to be much safer than stocks.

Curious about whether this investment strategy really worked, I hopped on Google and checked out one of the bond funds that the book raved about. The day I checked (which was in mid-May 2020), the stock market was still down about 15% from coronavirus-related volatility. How had this "safe" bond fund fared during this same time period? It was down 40%! This was a good reminder of the old adage that if something seems too good to be true (like 8% returns on a safe investment), it is.

In their book *The Investment Answer*, Daniel C. Goldie and Gordon S. Murray eloquently explain why you should not follow the advice of most Wall Street brokers and the financial press. Goldie and Murray explain that most investors incorrectly think that success comes from three things: (1) timing the market (entering during a trough and exiting during a peak), (2) choosing the best individual stocks, and (3) finding the best money manager to help you time the market and choose the best stocks. Goldie and Murray then explain that "these activities waste your time, cost you money, and reduce your return."

Agreed. You cannot time the market. No one can. You cannot choose the best individual stocks. No one can. And you cannot find a money manager who will do these things for you. Not in the long run. Sure, you may have short-term success on any one of these three things, but the odds are stacked against any of these techniques producing long-term success.

What about investing just a small amount of your portfolio in individual stocks? Although most experts recognize that low-fee index funds are a better bet than individual stocks, they often say it's okay to take a small portion of your portfolio and invest it in individual stocks.

I don't like this tactic. Think about it. Let's say you put 10% of your portfolio into a stock you think will perform well, like Amazon, Apple, or Tesla. In my view, the best-case scenario is that the stock tanks right after you invest in it.

Why is losing your money the best-case scenario? Because if you lose money, you'll see that it's not worth it to invest in individual stocks. You'll return to the research that shows that low-fee index funds are a wiser investment, and you'll likely fare much better in the long run.

If, on the other hand, the stock happens to do well, you'll feel rewarded for making such a genius choice to invest in it. In the book *Your Money and Your Brain*, Jason Zweig cites neurological research that finds that the human brain treats winning money the same way it treats cocaine. The brain literally becomes addicted to it. If this happens to you, you'll almost certainly end up investing much more than 10% of your portfolio in speculative stock picks, and you'll almost certainly end up losing much more money compared to what you would gain if you invested in low-fee index funds. It's better to stick with the data.

Where do I invest?

So now that you're interested in low-fee index funds, where do you get them? For an individual investor, three companies are best known for providing low-fee index funds with low expense ratios: Vanguard, Fidelity, and Schwab. (Note: I do not have any affiliation with any of these companies.) You can easily set up an account with any of them online.

Each of these three companies has its advantages. Many investors go with Vanguard because it is investor-owned, so they have a long track record of providing low fees that are in the best interests of investors. In fact, the founder of Vanguard, Jack Bogle, is largely responsible for the availability and popularity of low-fee index funds. His dedication to the everyday investor — you and me — has given him well-deserved hero status, and many investors show their devotion to Jack Bogle by investing only in Vanguard funds.

That said, Fidelity and Schwab also deserve a look. If you've decided that socially responsible investing is right for you then you may prefer to go with Fidelity, since it now offers socially responsible versions of all three of the low-fee index funds that most investors seek. And if you're looking to do your banking at the same place you do your investing, Schwab is known for offering an excellent checking account that won't charge you the fees that so many other banks charge. So you really can't go wrong with any of these three companies. Just pick one and go for it.

Mutual funds or ETFs?

Finally, when picking funds, I've mentioned only low-fee mutual funds so far in this chapter, but you should know that Exchange Traded Funds (ETFs) are a great choice as well.

In fact, for a regular taxable brokerage account, ETFs are often preferable. This is because ETFs are generally more tax efficient than mutual funds. Also, many ETFs have even lower expense ratios than low-fee index mutual funds. For instance, Vanguard's Total Stock Market Index Fund (VTSAX) has an expense ratio of 0.04, while the Vanguard Total Stock Market ETF (VTI) is only 0.03. Another benefit of ETFs is that there is no minimum investment. By contrast, many Vanguard mutual funds currently require an initial investment of $3,000.

That said, for a tax-advantaged account like a 401(k), IRA, or Roth IRA, there are two reasons that I personally prefer low-fee mutual funds over ETFs.

The first is that it's easier to set up automatic deposits with a mutual fund because you can invest an exact dollar amount (like $100 per paycheck). ETFs, on the other hand, usually require purchasing a specific amount of shares (so, for instance, if one share costs $170, then your $100 would not be able to buy any). Fortunately, this is changing, and many online companies are now moving toward allowing the purchase of partial shares.

The second reason I prefer mutual funds is that, depending on your brokerage firm, ETFs can incur commission fees when you purchase or sell them. Because ETFs can be purchased and sold during the day (whereas mutual fund transactions only occur at the end of each day), you might be tempted to make more trades with an ETF. As discussed throughout the chapter, you're usually better off with a long-term "buy-and-hold" investment strategy, rather than regularly trading funds.

That is why I prefer mutual funds for tax-advantaged accounts, but you can't go wrong either way.

27

ASSET ALLOCATION AND REBALANCING

W hat about asset allocation? This is actually the most important decision you make about your portfolio. You need to have a mix of domestic stocks, international stocks, and bonds. A low-fee index fund for each of those categories provides you with your basic three-fund portfolio.

Yes, you could add in lots of other index funds, or even an investment in gold or a real estate investment trust (REIT), but I tend to think that the simpler, the better, particularly when you're just starting out. If you go with a three-fund portfolio, the particular make-up of that mix (what percentage you assign to each of your three funds) is up to you. I'll try to provide some thoughts to consider in making your decision.

And whatever you decide, you're probably going to want to use periodic rebalancing to keep the appropriate mix.

Asset allocation

Your asset allocation should be simple and effective. Of course, you want it to maximize your returns. Everyone does. But don't let perfect get in the way of good. No asset allocation is ever going to be perfect. You should look for something that will work well and be simple to implement.

Let's start with the simplest portfolio: dividing your money evenly into a low-fee domestic stock index fund (33%), a low-fee international stock index fund (33%), and a low-fee bond index fund (33%). This ticks all the boxes — domestic stocks, international stocks, and bonds. And it's incredibly simple, particularly when it comes to rebalancing, as your goal is to always have an equal amount in each of these three funds.

This is the simple portfolio that William J. Bernstein recommends in *If You Can: How Millennials Can Get Rich Slowly*. It's not perfect, but it should perform well. And whatever you try to gain by seeking a better asset allocation is arguably not worth what you'll lose when you divert from the simplicity of the evenly divided three-fund portfolio.

Particularly if you're just starting out investing, this is a great portfolio to begin with. It gives you broad diversification and, because your money is evenly divided among three funds, it will help you learn what funds do better during which times.

That said, my personal preference based on everything I've read is to keep the bond portion of your fund lower than 33%. Unless you know you have more money than you could ever use, most savvy investors recommend keeping at least 75% of your portfolio in stocks (equities), with the remaining 10-25% in bonds.

When you are close to retirement, most investors want their portfolio to have a higher percentage of bonds, but even then you may want to keep it at only 25%.

A popular option for low-fee bond index funds is Vanguard's Total Bond Market Index Fund (VBTLX), but you should also consider Fidelity's Sustainability Bond Index Fund (FNDSX).

Note that some people would say that this portion of your portfolio should be kept in "cash and bonds," but I think that confuses savings with investments. Yes, you should keep some assets in cash. At least enough to cover a few months' worth of expenses. But cash is not an investment. At least not now.

If savings accounts and certificates of deposits (CDs) start offering interest rates of 5% or more — which has happened in the past, but not for many, many years — then you can start viewing that as part of your portfolio. And it should be grouped with your bonds, as these are collectively "fixed income" assets. But for now, it's easiest to think of your portfolio as just stocks and bonds.

If you went with a target-date retirement fund, you would probably start out with an allocation of at least 75% stocks. But in a traditional target-date fund, your bond investments would increase significantly as you approached retirement age. By retirement age, many standard portfolios would have moved you to around 50% bonds. The idea is that you want a more conservative portfolio as you near retirement since at that point you have fewer years to recover if the stock market dives.

The problem with the traditional target-date retirement fund approach is that, unless you have way more money than you'll ever need, it's actually riskier to lock in the low returns that bonds provide when you could make far more in stocks. If you want more information on why you should always keep at least 75% of your portfolio in stocks, look at Chapter 29 of *The Simple Path to Wealth* by J.L. Collins (First Edition). That chapter is titled "Withdrawal Rates: How Much Can I Spend Anyway?" It explains in detail the research behind the 4% safe withdrawal rate and cites recent studies that break down the historical performance of different asset allocations. The most interesting finding is that a portfolio of 75% stocks and 25% bonds, drawn down at 4% in the first year and then at a higher adjusted-for-inflation amount every following year, has historically had a 100% success rate over 30 years.

You might want to read that sentence again. Of course, this is a good time to remember that past performance does not guarantee future success. But this is about as close as you'll ever get to a sure thing in any reasonable investment strategy.

What is also interesting is that the success rate goes down with different asset allocations. A 100% stock allocation had a 98% success rate, and a 50% stock allocation had a 96% success rate. Granted, those are pretty amazingly high numbers too. But it's significant that the most secure allocation during retirement was 75% stocks and 25% bonds. That's good enough for me.

These numbers show that, despite conventional wisdom that bonds are always safer, it can actually be riskier to keep more than 25% of your portfolio in bonds.

This is all the truer when you take into account that you have no idea how long you're going to live. Sure, you can estimate it, but you could easily be off by a decade or more. If you end up needing to live off your nest egg for more than 30 years, a bond-heavy portfolio could hold you back. Stocks, on the other hand, have historically outperformed bonds over the long term, so keeping 75% of your portfolio in stocks will allow gains that are more likely to sustain you over the long term.

So if you agree that you want at least 75% of your portfolio in stocks, the question then becomes how much of the rest of your portfolio to allocate to bonds. This is something to discuss with a professional financial advisor, but here's one option to consider:

- Stage 1: Until age 40 or retirement (whichever comes earlier): 90% stocks, 10% bonds.
- Stage 2: From age 40 until retirement: 80% stocks, 20% bonds
- Stage 3: At retirement: 75% stocks, 25% bonds

You don't need to make it any more complicated than that. Unlike target-date retirement funds, there are only three different groups of asset allocations here. And if you're like me, and you failed to invest much of anything before age 40, you start at Stage 2, so you only have two asset allocations to worry about!

On a more positive note, if you retire at age 40 or earlier, you also only have two allocations to deal with, because you get to skip Stage 2 altogether. For early retirees, you would have 90% stocks and 10% bonds up until the day of retirement, and then you would reallocate your portfolio to 75% stocks and 25% bonds.

(Note, you would not want to do any of these conversions in just one day. You would want to do your research on how to make the transition between each stage.)

As for allocation within each category, you only need one bond fund. The best option is usually a low-fee index fund like VBTLX.

But for stocks, it's a little more complicated. Most financial advisors recommend that you have at least two stock funds so that you have some international exposure. In particular, you probably want to aim to have at least 25% of your stocks in international funds. In fact, you may want to consider having as much as 50% of your stocks in international funds.

Here is a sample portfolio for someone younger than 40 and not yet retired:

- 60% low-fee domestic stock index fund, such as:
    - Vanguard FTSE Social Index Fund Admiral Shares (VFTSX),
    - Fidelity US Sustainability Index Fund (FITLX), or
    - Vanguard Total Stock Market Index Fund (VTSAX)
- 30% low-fee international index stock fund, such as:
    - Fidelity International Sustainability Index Fund (FNIDX), or
    - Vanguard Developed Markets Index Fund Admiral Shares (VTMGX)
- 10% low-fee bond market index fund, such as:
    - Fidelity's Sustainability Bond Index Fund (FNDSX), or
    - Vanguard's Total Bond Market Index Fund (VBTLX)

Here is a sample portfolio for a 40-year-old:

- 55% low-fee domestic stock index fund, such as VFTSX, FITLX, or VTSAX
- 25% low-fee international index stock fund, such as FNIDX or VTMGX
- 20% low-fee bond market index fund, such as FNDSX or VBTLX

Here is a sample portfolio for someone at retirement:

- 50% low-fee domestic stock index fund, such as VFTSX, FITLX, or VTSAX
- 25% low-fee international index stock fund, such as FNIDX or VTMGX
- 25% low-fee bond market index fund, such as FNDSX or VBTLX

Regular rebalancing

Rebalancing your portfolio is another important aspect of asset allocation.

Whether you rebalance, and how often, depends on whether your funds are in a tax-advantaged account like a 401(k), IRA, or Roth IRA. Always check with your brokerage firm, but if you have money in a tax-advantaged account, then you can usually make transactions without any tax consequences. Thus, if you want to sell some of your stocks and buy more bonds or vice versa, it would not cost you anything to do this.

If, on the other hand, you have a regular taxable brokerage account, then you'll want to be more careful about rebalancing, as there could be significant tax consequences. For instance, if you're selling stocks because they have gained so much in value, and buying bonds to rebalance, you may owe capital gains taxes on that transaction. This still may be worth it, but you'll want to look more closely at whether to do this.

Assuming there are no costs to rebalancing, you will want to rebalance your portfolio once or twice a year and whenever there is a market change of 20% or more. For your annual or semi-annual rebalancing, pick a date like your birthday and check your portfolio on that date every year. Note that it's better to choose a date that is not the beginning of January, as stocks tend to be more in flux then.

Then, particularly if you can sell and buy without incurring any fees, you should rebalance to your targets. This rebalancing lets you sell high and buy low.

The same goes for rebalancing when there's a market change of 20% or more. So, for instance, if your portfolio aims for 80% stocks and 20% bonds, but then the market crashes and your stocks go down while your bonds go up, you may find yourself with too high a percentage of bonds. This is a great time to sell your high-priced bonds and buy more low-priced stocks. You're selling high and buying low, taking advantage of a time when stocks are on sale.

Rebalancing can also happen anytime you get extra money (like an inheritance, a tax refund, or a bonus). Check your portfolio and invest that extra money in whichever funds have fallen below their allocation. The Mad Fientist calls this "no-sell rebalancing." So, for instance, if your target is 20% bonds, but your bonds are underperforming relative to your stocks, and have fallen to 15%, you would put more money into your bonds. The idea is that bonds are "on sale" then because their prices have fallen.

This type of rebalancing — buying more of whatever has fallen behind — is a particularly good option for regular taxable brokerage accounts. Because you're only buying, and not selling, you do not have to worry about the tax consequences of sales.

A word of caution: buying low and selling high (which you'll do every time you rebalance) sounds easy, but is often very difficult, even for smart people like yourself. There have been several psychological studies that show that people do exactly the opposite when it comes to their investments. When a stock price goes down, people assume it's a losing bet and are inclined to sell. And when a stock price goes up, they figure it's a win and they should buy more of it.

In fact, a recent article noted that even the great mathematical genius Sir Isaac Newton made this exact mistake 300 years ago when he invested nearly all of his money in the South Sea Company at the peak of its share price. Thomas Levenson's article is called *Investors Have Been Making the Same Mistake for 300 Years: If Isaac Newton could lose all reason in the pursuit of riches, so can anyone else.* It's well worth a read so that you know that even the smartest among us are subject to the same psychological pressures to buy high and sell low when the data shows that you'd be far better off with the exact opposite approach.

Finally, let me address a question that occurred to me when I learned that, historically, the best long-term investment has been VTSAX or another low-fee index fund: if that's the best bet, then why not put all my money in that fund? What's the point of also investing in international stocks or buying bonds? This is a great question. After all, if I'm looking at three investment options, and one averages 10% per year, one 8%, and one 6%, why would I ever buy into the 8% or 6%? Why not put all of my money in the fund that averages 10%?

There are a few answers to this question.

First, a diverse asset allocation lowers your risk of significant losses. Remember that past performance is not a guarantee of future performance. Thus, while the U.S. stock market has historically done great, I would not want to have all my eggs in one basket.

Think of what 2020 brought when the coronavirus impacted different countries in vastly different ways. There are a number of world events that could lead to international markets faring far better than U.S. markets. This is why I think it's crucial to have a significant portion of your portfolio invested in international equities. And having bonds gives you another hedge against a bear market.

Second, a diverse asset allocation provides big benefits if you ever need to withdraw money unexpectedly. I'm not talking about panic selling. As we've discussed, you know not to sell when everyone else is. In fact, you know that's the best time to buy because stocks are on sale. You're going to ride it out rather than lock in losses.

That said, you may not have that luxury. A buy-and-hold strategy only works if you have the funds — outside of your investments — to pay for all of your expenses. Chances are, you will. But there's also a chance that something unexpected happens (for instance, you or a family member has a health issue, or you lose your job and cannot find another one), and this event may require far more funds than you have set aside for emergencies. While you might have planned on a buy-and-hold strategy for your investments, this may prove to be impossible.

If you end up needing to cash out some of your investments earlier than planned, you'll be glad to have a diverse asset allocation. That will allow you to make your withdrawals from whatever funds are performing best at that particular time, allowing you to sell high rather than sell low.

Third, believe it or not, many studies have shown that a diverse asset allocation generally fares better over the long run than simply investing in the best performing asset. This is a bit counterintuitive, but it's true.

There are a few reasons for this. One is that lower-performing investments such as bonds often have lower volatility, which can lead to larger gains when you factor in the effects of compounding. This is because a 20% gain one year, followed by a 10% loss the next year (which averages out to a 5% gain per year) leaves you with less money than a fund that consistently makes 5% each year.

I know that sounds strange, but the math bears it out. If, for instance, a $100,000 investment gains 20%, it goes to $120,000, but then a 10% loss brings it to $108,000. Meanwhile, the more stable fund would go from $100,000 to $105,000 and then to $110,250. So even though both investments have averaged a gain of 5%, the more stable investment made $2,250 more.

Fourth, diversification pays off because it allows you to take advantage of regular rebalancing of your portfolio (for instance, every six months or whenever there's a 20% change in any of your holdings). That means that you're consistently selling high (locking in gains) and buying low.

Again, this is not market timing. You don't care whether the market is going up or down. You're rebalancing regardless. Thus, in a bull market, you would sell stocks every six months, locking in gains as you convert those funds into bonds. And in a bear market, you would sell bonds every six months and buy more stocks while they're on sale. This diversification and rebalancing provide the golden goose of investing: greater gains at a lower risk.

Need a simpler solution?

Dealing with asset allocation and portfolio rebalancing is not for everyone. Even if you only have three funds and only reallocate once a year, you may find this process to be more work than you'd like. No problem. There's an even easier way to invest the smart way: target-date retirement funds. These are true "set it and forget it" investment funds. You pick your fund based on your anticipated retirement date, and then the fund manager rebalances the fund for you as you get closer to that date.

Personally, I don't use target-date retirement funds for two reasons. First, they always have higher expense ratios than buying your own mix of low-fee index funds. Second, they are usually more conservative (too high a portion of bonds relative to stocks) than most financial advisors recommend.

That said, one fund company, Vanguard, has gone a long way toward addressing both of these concerns. Their target-date retirement funds tend to have expense ratios in the 0.15% range, which is quite good. And they tend to have a larger share of stocks even as you get close to retirement. So if you want the simplest solution, you should take a look at target-date retirement funds.

That's asset allocation in a nutshell. It's not rocket science. In fact, it's pretty straightforward. Anyone can do it, and everyone should. Whether you have $5 to spare every month or $5,000, make sure you put aside as much money as possible and invest it wisely. Don't aim for perfection. That's impossible. But for most of us, all we need to do is pick an asset allocation, find corresponding low-fee index funds, and then use periodic rebalancing to keep us on track.

28

Make Regular CONTRIBUTIONS

O kay, you now know how to maximize your returns from investing. That puts you way ahead of most people.

But this knowledge won't do you any good if you don't put it into action. Remember that your returns are always a percentage of your total investments. You could have the best investment strategy in the world and it won't do you any good if you only put $100 into it.

Your investment strategy needs to include a plan for maximizing your contributions. Luckily, it's easier than ever to put in place a system of regular contributions.

All you need to do is set up automatic deductions from your paycheck and have those deductions invested either in an employer-sponsored retirement plan or your own brokerage account or both. Alternatively, if automatic deductions don't work for you, you can set up automatic contributions to your investment accounts that are timed for the day after each paycheck arrives.

The key word is automation. This money gets automatically invested every single time you get a paycheck. You're paying yourself first. This ensures that you make regular contributions every time you can.

Making regular automatic contributions means you don't have to have a budget. That's why some people refer to paying yourself first as a "reverse budget." You set aside what you need for retirement first, and then what's left is your budget for all other expenses. Yes, you can (and probably should) still create a budget within that budget to make sure you don't overspend on one thing and then get left without enough to pay whatever bill happens to arrive last. But if you're one of the many people who would rather get a root canal than a budget, then the pay yourself first principle is probably right for you.

Dollar-cost averaging

Another big advantage of regular, automatic contributions to your retirement: it takes advantage of something known as "dollar-cost averaging." This is a way of automatically buying more stocks when they're on sale.

Here's how it works. Let's say you set up an automatic deduction from your paycheck of $100 every two weeks. When your first $100 is invested in a low-fee index fund like FITLX, let's say the price is $20 per share. That means your $100 just bought you 5 shares. But then, two weeks later, markets plummet and the share price drops to $10. Your friends, who have not read this book, panic and pull all their money out of the stock market. This locks in all of their losses. You, however, are smart and know that after stock prices fall, they're on sale, and that's a time to buy, not sell. So you keep your money invested, and when your next $100 goes in, it buys you 10 shares — double what you got before!

So you bought $100 worth of $20 shares and then $100 worth of $10 shares. That means you paid $15 per share, right? Wrong. You did much better than that. Due to dollar-cost averaging, because your $100 bought you more shares when they were on sale, you ended up buying a total of 15 shares for $200, which means you only paid $13.33 per share! This is the beauty of regular automatic contributions to your investments.

One quick caveat to dollar-cost averaging: it only applies to regular contributions. Research shows that you should not apply the theory of dollar-cost averaging to lump sums (for instance, when you receive an inheritance or a big tax refund). Because the stock market goes up more often than it goes down, the research shows that lump sums should be invested immediately, rather than kept in cash and invested over a longer period of time.

So, for instance, if you inherit $1 million, you're usually better off investing it all right away rather than, for instance, putting in $100,000 every month over 10 months. The reason is that you're likely to lose more in interest from keeping so much cash in the bank (where it makes next to nothing). In other words, if you invest only $100,000 the first month, then you lose out on the potential gains you would get if you also invested the other $900,000. That loss usually outweighs any advantage you might get from dollar-cost averaging.

29

TAXES ARE NOT INEVITABLE

S
o we've now covered how to choose investments, how to choose your asset allocation and perform regular rebalancing, and how to set up automatic contributions. There's one important topic left: taxes.

This chapter is not about how to avoid taxes. And, as a reminder, I'm not a tax professional. There are lots of good tax professionals out there, and you should seek out professional advice on anything tax-related.

In this chapter, I'm just going to mention a few tax strategies that everyone should know about. These are simple ways to minimize your taxes — and thus maximize your investments.

The amazing Roth IRA and Roth IRA conversions

One of the best ways to minimize taxes is the amazing Roth IRA. The Roth IRA should be tax strategy #1 for most of us. There are income limitations, so not everyone can contribute to a Roth IRA. Also, for those who pay high taxes now and plan to make much less money during retirement, a Roth IRA may not make sense. But if you do qualify to make contributions to a Roth IRA, make sure you look into how to maximize them. You'll also want to consider whether you should put some of your other investments through Roth IRA conversions so you can make tax-free withdrawals in retirement.

When you set up an investment account, or make investments through an employer-sponsored account, you're not only deciding what investments to purchase, but you're also deciding what *type* of tax vehicle will host your investments.

There are three major types of tax vehicles for your investments:

Regular taxable accounts	Paid for with after-tax dollars.	Gains are taxed at withdrawal.
Tax-deferred accounts like a 401(k)	Paid for with pre-tax dollars.	Everything (original investment amount and any gains) taxed at withdrawal.
The amazing Roth IRA	Paid for with after-tax dollars.	No taxes at all at withdrawal!

Okay, the last type of account is not actually called the "amazing" Roth IRA. But it should be, as I'll explain in detail below.

Think of the tax vehicle as the container for your investments. Each tax vehicle is like a suitcase that holds all of the investments you put into it.

Suitcases are incredibly important. You would not want to pack ironed dress shirts or evening dresses in a duffel bag. The same goes for your investments. Each should be placed in an appropriate suitcase.

My family learned the importance of suitcases when we went on vacation one year and my mom realized that she had forgotten her bathing suit. We were already 30 minutes into our road trip, so we had a long family debate about whether to drive back home just for mom's bathing suit. It was the middle of winter, but we had all packed bathing suits because our "vacation" was really just a glorified hotel stay, where the only thing to do would be to swim in the hotel pool. We decided it was worth it to circle back so my mom could get her bathing suit.

The roads were icy, and our family minivan couldn't make it up the hill to our house. My mom hopped out and started walking. We waited for her to come back.

And waited. Why was it taking her so long just to grab a bathing suit?

Eventually, my mom crested the hill. She was slowly dragging an oversized suitcase. It turns out my parents had forgotten not just a bathing suit, but their entire shared suitcase!

You don't want to forget your suitcases when you put together your portfolio. Make sure you spend time figuring out which suitcases make the most sense for your investments. The tax implications are significant, and you'll want to make sure you get this right.

Many financial advisors focus on tax-deferred 401(k) plans. Tax-deferred investments have significant advantages, particularly for those who are currently in a high tax bracket.

If, for instance, you pay 30% in income taxes, then you can invest $10,000 in a tax-deferred plan for the price of $7,000 in an after-tax investment like a regular taxable account or a Roth IRA. Also, you can usually invest more money each year in tax-deferred investments (which are capped at $19,500 in 2021, or $26,000 if you're 50 or older) than in a Roth IRA (which is capped at $6,000 in 2021, or $7,000 if you're 50 or older). But I say "usually" because there are now a number of employers that offer a Roth 401(k) or something similar that allows you to contribute at the higher limits to a Roth! Many people are unaware of this option, but it's worth looking into because, for most investors, the Roth IRA is the way to go.

Why is the Roth IRA amazing? Let's say your employer offers a 401(k) or a 457 plan in both a traditional and Roth form. You probably know this already, but traditional retirement accounts work as follows: you get a tax deduction when you invest, but then have to pay taxes on everything — your investment and all of its gains — when you withdraw. The Roth, on the other hand, provides no tax deduction on your initial investment but allows withdrawals — of the investment and all of its gains — completely tax-free.

In 2021, for most investors, the maximum annual investment in a 401(k) or 457 plan is $19,500. Let's say you want to invest the maximum amount. Where do you put it — in the traditional fund or in a Roth?

A lot of books and articles recommend investing in a traditional retirement fund to get the tax deduction now. The theory is that you're probably in your prime earning years now and therefore in a higher tax bracket than you'll be when you retire. However, I think that advice is outdated, at least for those of us who have children.

If you have dependents, then you may be in the lowest tax bracket you'll ever be in. Recent changes to tax laws, as well as massive increases in federal spending in response to the coronavirus, make it far more likely that many of us will be in a higher tax bracket when we retire.

Let's start with some of the recent changes to the tax laws. For a married couple with three children and student loans, you can make $80,000 before you pay *anything* in income taxes. If you're in this category and you have the option of a Roth, you should invest in the Roth! This is the best of both worlds. Your tax bill remains at $0, and your investments and all of your returns will be tax-free!

So before you decide whether to do a traditional retirement investment or a Roth, you need to find out what your tax situation is this year. Fortunately, the IRS has an excellent tax estimator that is available here: https://apps.irs.gov/app/tax-withholding-estimator/.

Check out that website and play around with different calculations for the amount that you withhold in a 401(k) or 457 account. If, as in the above example, you have no income tax liability this year, then all your money should go into a Roth. On the other hand, if you're in a very high tax bracket this year, then you probably want to go for the immediate tax deduction.

Most likely, you fall somewhere in between. If you think you want to go for the tax deduction now, just make sure that you're actually getting a tax deduction. It may be that a $10,000 tax deduction brings your tax liability to $0, in which case you'd want to invest every dollar after that in a Roth.

What if your employer doesn't offer a Roth version of the 401(k) or 457? No problem. You can set up your own Roth, as long as you're below the adjusted gross income limits (around $200,000 for a married couple in 2021). And the amount you can invest is double for married couples because each spouse can have their own Roth IRA. So if you and your spouse are 50 or older, you can put $14,000 in your Roth accounts every year!

The best part about a Roth is that it's tax-free forever. This means that if you end up being in a higher tax bracket when you retire, you don't have to worry about it!

And there are lots of ways you could end up in a higher tax bracket. I'll mention three here.

First, you may lose lots of tax deductions you currently have. For instance, if you're not on track to retire early, you'll lose tax deductions for things like student loan interest and, most significantly, for any dependent children you have.

Second, you may end up earning much more in retirement than you earn now. For instance, if you get into real estate or your hobby of catfish noodling lands you a high-paying TV gig as the star of a new show on catfish noodling. (If you don't know what that is, look it up. And watch some YouTube videos of it. You're welcome.)

Third, even if your income is less in retirement, the tax brackets could be far higher than they are now. It is worth noting that, as I write this in 2021, the U.S. is at historically low tax rates. Tax rates used to be as high as 90%! And the U.S. is simultaneously spending more than we ever have before, particularly since the coronavirus hit.

Something has to give, and it's a good bet that we'll see higher tax rates in the near future. In fact, the historically low tax rates we're experiencing now are already set to automatically rise in 2025. You avoid all of this risk by investing in a Roth IRA now.

The Roth has many other benefits as well. I'll just mention three:

- **Roths have more flexibility than other retirement accounts when it comes to withdrawals.** In particular, you can withdraw your contributions (the amount you invested, but not its earnings) before you reach retirement age, without paying any taxes or penalties. You can also withdraw from a Roth both contributions and earnings for buying your first home.

- **Withdrawing from a Roth IRA does not increase your taxes on Social Security payments.** Just about every other income stream or investment withdrawal in retirement will increase the amount you're taxed on Social Security.

- **Roths are passed on to your heirs tax-free.** This has enormous benefits and greatly simplifies the process your heirs will go through in settling your estate.

Okay, at this point, you're probably convinced that the Roth IRA truly is amazing. But what if you're already a good way into your retirement investing? If that's you, then you might be thinking about Adam Sandler's line from *The Wedding Singer* that this is all information "that could've been brought to my attention YESTERDAY!"

Don't worry — I've got you covered. There's a tax strategy called a Roth IRA conversion that lets you take traditional IRA accounts and convert them to Roths. I won't explain it in detail, but the basic idea is that, if you're willing to "pay taxes" now, you can convert your retirement accounts to Roths that will then be tax-free forevermore. I put quotes around the phrase "pay taxes" because, if you time your conversions right, you might be able to turn your accounts into Roths without ever paying taxes at all. For instance, if you retire early and convert to a Roth IRA in a year when your earned income is low enough, you may not have any tax liability at all for this conversion. If you're interested in this, you should do your research and consult with a tax professional.

The Mad Fientist has an excellent article on how to minimize tax liability through Roth IRA conversions. It's called *Traditional IRA vs Roth IRA*, and you can find it at madfientist.com.

Health Savings Accounts, tax-gain harvesting, and tax-loss harvesting

The Mad Fientist has also written a detailed series of articles on other tax-advantaged investments like the Health Savings Account, and how to use tax-gain harvesting and tax-loss harvesting to minimize your tax liability on other investments. The Mad Fientist explains those topics far better than I ever could, so you'll want to read his articles, particularly if you're already maxing out your contributions to all of your other tax-advantaged retirement accounts.

For instance, the Health Savings Account provides a way for certain investors (those who have qualifying high-deductible healthcare plans) to invest pre-tax dollars for later use for health-related expenses. What's amazing about Health Savings Accounts is that the withdrawals are entirely tax free. So, for those who qualify, these accounts can be even better than a Roth! While both allow tax-free withdrawals, Roth investments are funded with after-tax money, while Health Savings Accounts are funded with pre-tax money.

Tax-gain harvesting and tax-loss harvesting are other strategies to look into for your regular taxable investment accounts. These strategies allow you to take advantage of years when your portfolio drops and years when it gains, to minimize the amount of taxes you'll ultimately owe when you make withdrawals.

Maximizing charitable donations

You may also want to look into how to minimize taxes when donating to your favorite charities. The best way to maximize a charitable donation is to get your company to match whatever you donate. Many companies do. Make sure to ask if there is any chance your company might match charitable donations. And tax strategies can also help. What I love about this is that it allows you to give even more to worthy causes. Again, you'll need to work with a tax professional on this, but the basic idea is to use pre-tax dollars, rather than after-tax dollars, for your charitable giving.

For instance, if you want to donate $10,000 to the Save the Wallabies Fund, you might actually need $15,000 of income to make that donation. That's because if you pay 33% in taxes, then you need $15,000 of pre-tax money to make a $10,000 payment. If, however, you could pay with pre-tax money, then all $15,000 would go toward saving those adorable little marsupials.

An easy way to do this is to set up a Donor Advised Fund. This allows you to take an immediate tax deduction for the amount you invest. That investment then hopefully grows, and all of the growth in the investment is also tax free. Then when you want to make a donation, you request that the fund send a specific amount to a specific charitable organization.

It's a "request" because, technically, the money is no longer yours. Once you donate it to the Donor Advised Fund, it belongs to that fund. You can't ever get it back and you can't demand that the money be used in any particular manner. But you can make requests, and these funds are specifically designed to honor those requests. A blogger known as the Physician on FIRE has written an excellent article on the details of setting up a Donor Advised Fund. It's called *The Donor Advised Fund: A Smarter Way to Give*, and you can find it at physicianonfire. com.

So next time you're thinking about writing a big check to your favorite cause, look into whether you could set up a Donor Advised Fund. This would allow you to make an even bigger impact by using pre-tax money rather than after-tax money.

CONCLUSION

We've covered a lot of ground in this book. Over the next few months, you may find yourself needing to flip back to particular sections to reread them. (As a reminder, if you want an up-to-date checklist of all 17 of the "Free Money Tips" that appear in this book, you can download it for free at personalfinanceauthor.com.)

Remember that no matter how complicated personal finance may seem, it's really quite simple. To improve your financial situation, there are only two levers you can pull. One is to make more. The other is to spend less.

This book has given you many ideas on how to pull each lever. An idea plus $5 will get you a cup of coffee. I'm kidding, of course. You only need an idea plus a quarter to get a great cup of coffee at home.

Now that you've learned these ideas for how to make more and spend less, you need to take action. Go back to the table of contents and choose one way you'll make more money this week. Then choose one way you'll spend less.

Do the same next week and the week after.

The next thing you know, your finances will start looking much better. As you make more and spend less, you'll see your bank account growing. You may then want to reread the chapters on how to invest wisely.

As your finances improve, you may discover that you're able to achieve financial independence and retire early. Or at least relatively early.

And one more thing. If your dad is like mine, or if you have anyone else in your family who makes financial mistakes all the time, cut them some slack. Don't try to set them straight — that never works. But you might want to jot down some notes about everything they did wrong. It could make for a great book.

Thank You and a Request

Your time is valuable. Thank you for spending some of that time reading my book. Whatever your thoughts on my book, it would mean the world to me if you would take a minute to leave an honest review of it on Amazon, Goodreads, and anywhere else. Thank you!

Get the Free Bonus Checklist

If you didn't already download it, remember to check out the up-to-date checklist of all 17 of the "Free Money Tips" that appear in this book. You can download it for free at: **personalfinanceauthor.com**

ADDITIONAL RESOURCES

've attempted to make my book the closest thing to one-stop shopping that you can get. But if you want more, there is plenty out there. Below are some lists of books, websites, blogs, and podcasts that are worth your time.

Two important notes:

(1) All of these resources have good ideas in them, but most (in fact, prob-ably all of them) also contain things I would not recommend. In fact, some of these resources contain the very things I recommend you *not* do. Also, some of these resources have viewpoints and stereotypes that, in my opinion, are no longer appropriate in today's day and age. Please know that I do not endorse these resources — I just list them because I think they contain *some* valuable information.

(2) Make sure to get the most updated version of each of these resources. While some aspects of personal finance are timeless, other ideas are ever-evolving. Do not try to save a few dollars by buying an out-of-date version if a newer version is available. Even the newest version is some-times behind the times. For instance, one of these books was updated in 2018 and yet still contained a reference to "car phones." Really, David Bach? Does the original version talk about fax machines? So get the latest version you can, and enjoy!

Books

A Random Walk Down Wall Street, by Burton G. Malkiel
Broke Millennial, by Erin Lowry
Choose FI, by Chris Mamula, Brad Barrett, and Jonathan Mendonsa
Don't Retire Broke, by Rick Rodgers
Financial Freedom, by Grant Sabatier
Go Big Fast and Do More Good, by Ido Leffler & Lance Kalish
Go Green, Live Rich, by David Bach & Hilary Rosner
How to Invest for Retirement, by Anthony S. Park
How to Manage Your Money When You Don't Have Any, by Erik Wecks
How to Retire Early, by Robert Charlton
How to Stop Living Paycheck to Paycheck, by Avery Breyer
I Will Teach You to be Rich, by Ramit Sethi

If You Can: How Millennials Can Get Rich Slowly, by William J. Bernstein
Income for Life, by Joseph DiSalvo and Marie Madarasz
Meet the Frugalwoods, by Elizabeth Thames
Millionaire Teacher, by Andrew Hallam
Money Honey, by Rachel Richards
Passive Income, Aggressive Retirement, by Rachel Richards
Quit Like a Millionaire, by Kristy Shen and Bryce Leung
Rich Dad's Retire Rich, Retire Young, by Robert Kiyosaki
Set for Life, by Scott Trench
Smart Couples Finish Rich, by David Bach
Stacked, by Joe Saul-Sehy and Emily Guy Birken
The $100 Startup, by Chris Guillebeau
The 4-Hour Work Week, by Tim Ferriss
The Four Pillars of Investing, by William Bernstein
The Little Book of Common Sense Investing, by John Bogle
The Millionaire Next Door, by Thomas Stanley & William Danko
The Path, by Peter Mallouk
The Simple Path to Wealth, by J.L. Collins
The Smartest Investment Book You'll Ever Read, by Daniel R. Solin
The Tax Bomb in Your Retirement, by Josh Scandlen
The Total Money Makeover, by Dave Ramsey
The Truth About Money, by Ric Edelman
What You Should Have Learned About Money But Never Did, by Sophia Bera
Why Didn't They Teach Me This in School? by Cary Siegel
Work Optional, by Tanja Hester
Your Money or Your Life, by Vicki Robin & Joe Dominguez

Websites & Blogs

A Purple Life: https://www.apurplelife.com
ChooseFI: https://www.choosefi.com/
Fiology: https://www.fiology.com/
Get Rich Slowly: https://www.getrichslowly.org/
Mad Fientist: https://www.madfientist.com/
Mr. Money Mustache: https://www.mrmoneymustache.com/
The Military Guide: https://the-military-guide.com/

Podcasts

Afford Anything
BiggerPockets Money
Mad Fientist
Real Estate Rookie
Stacking Benjamins

ACKNOWLEDGMENTS

This book would not have happened without the help of many people.

I'm grateful to all of the authors and podcast hosts who have created helpful information about every aspect of personal finance and investing. In particular, the *BiggerPockets Money Podcast* and its hosts Mindy Jensen and Scott Trench introduced me to many of the ideas in this book. And I owe a special thanks to Mindy Jensen for writing such a wonderful foreword!

My reviewers and editors provided feedback that greatly improved every page of this book. I'm particularly grateful to MK Williams, Ashly Baugh, Crystal Parker Duffy, Julie Greb, Elijah Hawkes, Lourdes White, Amber Sauer, David Baughier, Stephen Baughier, Emily Guy Birken, my sister Heather Yountz, and my partner for reviewing the initial draft and providing helpful overarching suggestions to make this a much better book. Thank you also to my excellent graphic designer, Brian Prendergast at Brian P. Graphic Arts, and to all of my amazing kids for their support and contributions! I'm also grateful to many other early readers and my excellent editor Melanie Underwood for their close reviews. Any remaining errors are mine alone.

Finally, my parents deserve enormous thanks for letting me publish the many entertaining stories about my dad. Oh, and they also deserve thanks for parenting me. I wouldn't be who I am without their unending love, dedication, care, guidance, and even occasional wisdom. If I can provide my kids with anything near what my parents have given me, I'll consider it a success.

INDEX

About the Author

Kyle Landis-Marinello lives in Vermont with his fantastic partner, three wonderful kids, and an amazing dog. He is a practicing attorney, specializing in environmental and energy law. He received a master's degree in environmental law from Vermont Law School and a law degree from the University of Michigan, where even his free time was spent on study-related activities like being an editor of the *Michigan Law Review*. (This was before kids, so he didn't know what else to do with his time.) When he turned his research skills toward personal finance and investing, he learned how to improve his family's finances by $300,000 in one year. This did not come from being wealthy or from compromising his values. This $300,000 change came from receiving forgiveness of federal student loans, refinancing a home and private student loans, and other methods to make more, spend less, and invest wisely. His passions are family, friends, kayaking, frisbee, board games, comic books, and writing. He can be reached through the contact link at his website: **personalfinanceauthor.com**

KURTBUDLIGER.COM

www.ingramcontent.com/pod-product-compliance
Lightning Source LLC
Chambersburg PA
CBHW071216210326
41597CB00016B/1835